Praise

Stop Struggling and Start Living

▲

"In our time this is going to be a very important book for many who are looking for answers. Presented with an intriguing story, it challenges many of the old paradigms of life, but is clear in its guidelines and delivers on the promise of true self-help. A book that will be read and read again."

—Dan Poynter, Author of more than 100 books, Para Publishing

▲

"The brilliant writing style and uncanny expertise with which the author has woven her wisdom into universal law to create this captivating story, is simply enthralling. She manages to lead the reader along the path of self discovery in a way that has profound implications on a personal and professional level. *Stop Struggling and Start Living* ranks up there with the absolute best and in a time where I found myself at a low point professionally, it opened wonderful doors. I have given Elfreda's book to every employee in my company and all my family members. This is the self-help and inspirational book that everyone should read."

Merle Ballaigues, President of Thomas International North America

▲

"'Everything is energy' is the powerful message of Elfreda's book, so insightfully written that the Rules were like old friends as she introduced them in her informal and relaxed style. I knew some of this stuff—we all do, but found myself awakening through her writing, and, through her inspiration I began to put the Rules into practice—with outstanding results!"

—Sylvia McMurtry, NostalgiaBooks, Port Credit

"*Stop Struggling and Start Living* crossed my path at a time when I was struggling like an animal in a leg trap. I was negotiating the renewal of an employment contract and feeling very sorry for myself, unappreciated and over a financial barrel. This book gave me a tough love message that shook my world up. It wasn't overnight magic, but in the year that followed, people have rallied to my support and attitudes have changed dramatically. I rediscovered excitement in my work and I'm having fun again!"

—Michael Worsfold, President of Partnering Designs Inc.

▲

"Elfreda Pretorius has hit a homerun with her book, *Stop Struggling and Start Living.* Through the medium of storytelling she masterfully reveals how to be successful on every level, if we play by the Rules. If you're tired of the old promises that don't work or you don't understand, this book is a catalyst for real and lasting change. If you care about yourself and your children, it is a must read."

—Tony Davies, Author of the handbook *Get Out of the Bowl— The Keys to Universal Law* and Keynote Speaker, Business & Personal Coach: Momentum Business Strategists

▲

"In a time of social unrest, political upheaval and religious turmoil, Elfreda Pretorius invites us to ask ourselves, through conversations with her characters, to have faith in our own individual essence, to create our own destiny thus impacting the greater whole of the universe and all things in it. This book is a gift to mankind. Brilliantly told by a talented author."

Sandy Smeenk, Oakville, Ontario

"The magic and allure of this author is the frankness of her approach and the honesty and sincerity with which she shares her knowledge. Like Sam in the story, I was a totally unaware of the powerful creative nature I was born with and could implement. Learning this has unleashed immeasurable happiness and freedom which I didn't know was at the tips of my fingers."

—Susan M. Nicholas, Reiki Master

▲

"I finally discarded the shackles of guilt and I am free for the first time in 42 years. The conversational style made the learning so easy. This is simply a wonderful book that everyone should read."

—Beth Livingstone, Niagara Falls

▲

"Imagine creating the life you want and deserve by reading just one book? Stop Struggling and Start Living is a ground-breaking work that simplifies concepts of conscious living to enable phenomenal transformation in the reader's life. There is no doubt that the author writes from a perspective of experience. Inspirational and life changing!"

Lisa Rice, Classical Homeopath, Bowen Therapist, R.N.C.

▲

"I was amazed at how Pretorius' compelling story beckoned me to read on, rediscover and reassess my life strategies. Surprising, convincing and satisfying, it clarifies many of life's challenges to happiness and removes roadblocks to personal success. I recommend it to anyone who wants to improve the quality of their life, their personal relationships, as well as their relationship to the world we live in."

—Susan Hayden, Professor of Visual Merchandising and Marketing, Sheridan Institute of Technology and Higher Learning and Owner of Visual Marketing Primitive/Figurative Fine Art

"Thank you for writing a book which highlighted the incredible role of learning how to choose a response. It breathed new life into our relationship and marriage."

James McAllister, Manchester, UK

"*Stop Struggling and Start Living* provided me with the skill set I needed to overcome years of depression. I learnt how to focus, to control my responses and to think positively. My most important achievement was to stop thinking of myself as a victim. I now know how my personal energy affects my life and my relationships with others."

—Michael, Toronto, Canada

"Wow! I stopped complaining. I can't believe what a nag I must have been to others. I am responsible for my life in every respect. That set me free—for the first time. I have no more excuses."

—Ana du Toit, Paris, France

"The human spirit begins to soar, when truth is discovered that opens the door for higher understanding. This book embodies the reality of the ever-evolving consciousness and awareness of the human being. It consists of powerful tools to help us cope with all of life's challenges. Everybody should know the Rules of the Game!"

—John Harricharan, Author of *When You Can Walk On Water, Take the Boat* and *Morning Has Been Coming, All Night Long*

Stop Struggling

and

Start Living

The Rules of the Game

ELFREDA PRETORIUS

DreamTime Publishing, Inc.

DreamTime Publishing, Inc., books are available at special quantity discounts for bulk purchases for sales promotions, premiums, fund raising, and educational needs. For additional information, please contact us at **www.DreamTimePublishing.com**.

Library of Congress Cataloging-in-Publication Data

Pretorius, Elfreda.
    Stop struggling and start living : the rules of the game / Elfreda Pretorius. — 1st ed.
      p. cm.
    Rev. ed. of: Rules of the game : how to overcome struggle and start living.
    Includes bibliographical references.
    ISBN-13: 978-1-60166-010-7 (trade pbk. : alk. paper)
    1. Conduct of life—Fiction. I. Title.

    PR9199.4.P754S76   2007
    823'.92—dc22

                        2007006322

Trademarks used herein are for the benefit of the respective trademark owners.

This book was previously published as *Rules of the Game: How to Overcome Struggle and Start Living.*

Branding, website, and cover design for DreamTime Publishing by
    Rearden Killion * www.reardenkillion.com
Illustrations by Willem Pretorius * www.willempretorius.com
Text layout and design by Gary A. Rosenberg * www.garyarosenberg.com

Contents

Foreword

It is an honor and a privilege to have been asked to write the fore-word for this book. Reading Sam's story was an amazing experience for me, and I encourage you to not only read it yourself, but to pur-chase it as gifts for those you love. I think that this book will strongly affect every reader, and the total impact of the words will give them the strength to overcome their demons, the freedom to follow their heart, and the courage to live their dreams.

I was overwhelmed by various emotions as I followed the story, and I was intensely involved as it revealed the journey of a man through his darkest time toward the light. I found the story heart wrenching at times, warm at others, but in the final analysis, tremendously uplifting. I was totally engrossed in the words and awed by the skill with which Elfreda weaved the secrets to the Rules of the Game, and lessons to living a happy life, into each chapter.

When I first met Elfreda Pretorius, I was struck by her smile and the energy that seemed to enter the room with her. I had heard her referred to as "The Energy Lady," a person who strongly believed in, and taught, the Energy Principles of the universe. People told me that her message was powerful. However, as I sat through that first seminar,

I was not prepared for the passion with which she tells her story and delivers her wisdom. It was amazing. She brought that same passion and energy to this book. I found myself constantly shouting, "Yes!" in my mind. I finished the book, feeling relieved that all the answers were there, and inspired by the fact that they were simple and easy for me to follow.

I admire her ability to write such a beautiful, spellbinding, and moving story that at the same time, delivers an extraordinary message, a message that will help people to understand forgiveness, compassion, and the power of inner direction.

The book may upset some people, and its frankness may even cause anger in a few. But ultimately the truth in her words cannot be ignored. When all is said and done, it will create an awakening in those who read its pages. Many people wander through life searching for answers, and finding only empty promises in the religions, self-help groups, and self-help books that they explore. These individuals especially, will find comfort in the pages of this book. I think it is a book that will be read and reread by people who want to truly grasp the lessons and start their own journey toward a better life.

I encourage you to read this book with an open mind. I think that, regardless of your religious beliefs, you too, can embrace the teachings in this book and enrich your life.

In recommending this book, I believe that I am meeting part of my mission in life, to bring hope to the people around the world. I praise Elfreda, for sharing her insights and lessons with all of us, through the spiritual wisdom of this book. I thank her for being a teacher, a healer, and a friend.

Judy Suke, Waterdown, Ontario, Canada
President, Triangle Seminars, Professional Speaker,
Entertainer, and Author, Distinguished Toastmaster,
Member of National Speakers Association

Special Tributes

My deepest gratitude goes to the four men with whom I share my life:

John: for your unconditional love and unwavering support

Niko: for relentlessly demonstrating dedication and focus

Wimmie: for graciously agreeing to teach me

Charles: for stubbornly insisting I share in your joy of living

For my editor, Kathryn Hughes, whose careful eye for detail will give you a better experience with this book.

For all her support I am deeply indebted to my good friend, Judy Suke, who also wrote the foreword to *Stop Struggling and Start Living*. Often referred to as Canada's own Loretta LaRoche and author of *Life Can Be Funny—Tips to Get Through It,* Judy is an inspired speaker whose goal it is "to bring humor and hope to the world."

Author's Note

The characters in this story are purely fictional and bear no resemblance to anyone the author knows presently or has met in the past. The location of Table Mountain, Devil's Peak, and the cable car to the top of the mountain is accurate; creative license, however, was taken with regards to the actual physical location of buildings, paths, plants, and trees to facilitate the flow in conversation between the main characters, Aaron and Sam.

Introduction

*I*n the years that I have shared the principles of *Stop Struggling and Start Living* in seminars or in private counseling sessions, I was often asked: "Why don't you write a book?"

There is a time for everything, and when the time for writing the book came, there was no stopping the flow of it. The book just gushed out of me.

On a personal level, writing *Stop Struggling and Start Living* was an awe-inspiring experience, a deeply moving and creative journey that led me consciously into recesses of my mind that opened with great clarity and focus. Some of these places I had only before visited in dreams and visions, and I was both humbled and astonished at the unwavering "knowing" as I dealt with several of the contentious and sensitive philosophical concepts.

If you are overwhelmed by emotional, mental, or financial struggle, I wrote this book for you. Even if you just feel a constant pressure, or believe that you deserve more than what you presently have—be it in love, material goods, or understanding—I wrote this book for you. We have a birthright to happiness, and by understanding the Rules of the Game, we can learn how to overcome constant, needless struggle.

When we struggle, we don't really live; struggle sucks the life out of us, on all levels. If you expect to struggle, then that is what you will get. But you can learn to choose and expect happiness—then you will create that.

The purpose of the book is further to assist those who understand that growth and self-development is an intensely personal journey, and without a doubt, a personal effort.

It is a solitary path, often a very lonely one, but the destination leads far beyond the boundaries of this planet.

If you follow Sam through his struggle and his inevitable journey toward the Light, it is my sincere wish that you too, will make this transition.

My hope is that you will begin to take the power and control over your own life back, and above all, see the beauty that is inside of you and all others.

If you look closely, you will recognize the clues, you'll see the fingerprints, and you'll be able to follow the footprints as they are revealed to you, one by one in your own life.

If you internalize only one of these rules, I know your life will improve.

My wish for you is that you will claim what is yours.

Above all, I hope you choose happiness, for it cannot choose you.

Elfreda Pretorius
Oakville, Canada.

Beautiful
Table Mountain

*T*able Mountain is located within the southern tip of Africa, close to where the warm Indian and cold Atlantic oceans converge. It is majestic and breathtaking and for centuries has been a silent warning to ships and sailors from afar of the treacherous waters into which they were about to enter.

In the city of Cape Town, where many make a living in the shadows of her feet, the mountain reigns supreme—she completely dominates everything; she cannot be overlooked. The mountain is everywhere.

Awe inspiring, beautiful, and dangerous, the mountain is also secretive and mysterious. In the summer months when the South Easter winds begin to blow, she reaches up to the clouds to pull down a cloak of fog and mist. She then drapes this "tablecloth" over her flat surface, stretching from the south all the way to the north, and hides herself in the sky. This is where we meet Sam and Aaron.

▲　▲　▲

The Mountain

*H*e hesitated briefly in the doorway, taking in the expensive paintings on the walls, the solid mahogany table, and the three seated around it. He smelled the aroma of strong coffee, but knew it wasn't for him. The atmosphere felt paper-thin. An uncontrollable shiver ran down his spine.

The lawyer cleared his throat. Sam saw his lips moving, but heard a roaring silence. He felt the urge to laugh. It was just so unbelievable that this was happening to him, this on top of everything else. He sensed the drone of subdued voices from around the table, but saw the hospital, saw her, saw how that was beyond repair. He forced his thoughts back to the farce being played out in front of him.

The lawyer mouthed meaningless clichés: "performance, economic realities, globalization, corporate survival," etc., while Sam stared at his supervisor, surreptitiously paging through documents. *I'm taking the fall for you, you bastard.* He, too, avoided looking at Sam. But in their averted faces Sam read the same message—failure.

They all looked up together, startled, when he suddenly stood. He didn't care. He wasn't playing their game any longer. He turned on his heel and left the room without taking his jacket. Someone called his name, but he didn't respond. He kept walking, ignoring the elevator, deliberately choosing the stairway. He needed to feel each step he took.

He was suffocating. He needed to get out. *Out of what?* He needed to get away. *But where would he go, and without her?* His heart felt like lead.

He stumbled to his car in the underground parking lot and opened the window as he emerged into the street, hoping that the late-summer sounds of the city could offer him a point of connection with himself, with anything, but he registered only muffled noise. He drove around aimlessly.

At a red light, he leaned his forearms on the steering wheel, watching the people hustling across the road in front of him. They were rushing; brusquely shouldering their way through, anxious to get somewhere else.

Where? Where are they all going in such a hurry? Why does anyone rush to get anywhere? To please others, to make an impression, to be thought important? Is anyone free? Is there anyone who does not grovel or bend to please another?

He closed his eyes. *Everyone looked so unhappy. What was the point of it all? How do you lose the most important years of your life, and still think of living as worthwhile? Failure.*

In the same moment, Sam saw the mountain. He had lived in Cape Town for over twenty years, but had never been anywhere close to it. As the light turned, thought became deed; he gunned the engine and turned the wheel. To Table Mountain—*perfect.*

He bought a ticket and waited nervously with a group of Indian and Chinese tourists as the cable car banged its way into the berth, then glided to a standstill. The door slid open; he entered and chose a seat far away from everyone else. He kept his eyes on his black dress shoes and hid his face in his hands, feeling the uncomfortable itch of two-day-old stubble. He was still in the same clothes he had worn to the hospital the day before . . . the day before . . . His shirttail was hanging out; he had forgotten to shave earlier. *So what? What does it matter now?* He squeezed his eyes shut.

The cable car journey was advertised as "less than five minutes," but the panic had already begun. His stomach heaved at the thought of the abyss below him.

As soon as it cleared the berth, the car would slowly begin to spin around, providing visitors a full view of the mountain and bay area. Sweat beads formed around Sam's mouth and he felt the panic in waves. *Why did I choose the mountain?* He felt himself perspiring profusely, breathing shallowly through his mouth. *Anywhere but here . . .* The car began swinging wildly in the wind.

As it slowly built momentum, the car stabilized and gently started rotating, gliding easily up the familiar terrain of thick cables, toward the flat surface of the mountaintop. As they climbed higher and higher up the rock face, Sam's terror rose. He couldn't move, couldn't look. The sweet fragrance of the mountainside plants and shrubs nauseated him. *Thank God no one notices. Mountains are dangerous places. Mountains kill people.* He sat frozen. *Planes crash into mountains. People get lost and are never found. And others fall off the face of the earth by leaning over too far.*

There it was! No more failure.

The sense of relief made him dizzy. The group's chatter reached a crescendo of screams and gasps as the car twirled toward the rock face. Then it sailed expertly, just in time, into the berthing area of the mountain summit. Sam kept his eyes on his shoes. It was a warm day, but he was shivering.

"Sir?" A friendly voice, polite. Sam looked up into the smiling face hidden partially behind dark-tinted sunglasses; a hand was being extended toward him—the only person left sitting.

"Thank you," Sam said, ignoring the gesture. Keeping his head down, he stepped onto the concrete platform. He needed to find the edge, a cliff . . . *No, not yet. I can take my time. There's no one I have to please. No one left to remind me what a loser I am. I have my own schedule now.* He drifted toward the restaurant.

Later, he watched a group of suits emerge from the conference hall area of the restaurant, laughing and congratulating each other. *Arranging a big important deal in the sight of God? Right here, at the tip of Africa, in the clear blue sky? Wow, that's sure to make you immortal.*

In the little shop, Sam shuffled through the postcards with their magnificent aerial views: the mountain awash in sunlight; the mountain draped in a cloak of mist and fog. Postcards mailed from here would bear the Table Mountain stamp. *Like getting a postcard from the clouds, from God. From God? There is no God. And I'm not mailing anything to anyone.*

When the horn sounded to call the last of the visitors for the final descent, Sam had already moved out of sight, walking toward the furthest cliff. No one counted the visitors. The horn sounded insistently again—notice of the last car's departure down the mountain. But Sam was already climbing a path leading to a small hill, and thence to the cliff celebrated on the many postcards.

Why this? Why now? Was it what happened in the boardroom today? Was it the death of the child? Was it losing her? The baby died, but he had to give her up to life. Was that it? Why was this so hard for him? The miracle of their first meeting flashed briefly through his mind, but he pushed away the memory. *Anything. I'll take anything, any meaning.* He looked up at the sky and saw the first clouds beginning to move in. "I don't think you're anywhere out there, God!" he shouted, surprised to hear the rage in his voice.

There was no point to anything at all; he just didn't want to do it any longer. He needed to end all the pain and the terrible guilt. The mountain had called him, and he had responded. He kept his eyes on the path in front of him, and picked up his pace a little, eager now for the resolution.

At the summit plateau, Sam paused to catch his breath, surprised at arriving so quickly. He stood about ten feet away from the cliff edge, and then gasped as he looked down. He quickly turned to face away from it.

The first stirrings of the southeasterly breeze cooled his clammy skin. Soon it would gather momentum and force, driving the dark clouds and heavy fog before it, weaving the mountain's cloak of mystery. Sam's thoughts began to drift. *No, let's not waste any more time.*

He turned slowly to face the horizon and began to shuffle his way forward. He sensed the abyss waiting a few feet away from him. Spasms of nausea gripped him, and he struggled to steady himself. He kept his gaze fixed straight ahead and began breathing deeply. Then he was standing on the edge of the cliff—empty, calm, watching himself dispassionately.

The setting sun lingered wistfully on the horizon. Soon it would roll under the earth with a careless shrug and rise somewhere else; perhaps in a place where people preferred living over dying. Far away, the waves crashed onto the rocks with dull repetition. He knew the ocean was not directly beneath him, but he imagined he could hear it. He imagined the waves tracing a thin, white line along the coast, like the unsteady hand of a child learning to draw.

The nausea rose again, briefly, but again he fought to control it. *God, this is so high!* And then he felt a strange exhilaration. *I've come this far without turning back! I'm finally here. It was meant to be.*

"Are you quitting the game?" A voice, soft and deep, with just the faintest hint of curiosity.

His body stiffened with shock. Then he steadied himself. *Of course! I'm hallucinating. But nothing is going to stop me now. Nothing.*

"When you take another step forward, you will not fly." The same voice—deliberate, calm, deep, detached.

My mind is trying to trick me. But the voice? it sounds so real. Sam hesitated, confused. "Fuck." He swore under his breath, gritting his teeth. *I'm not in the mood for miracles. And it's too little, too late.* Sam felt the cold wind on his face as he carefully spread his arms, determined to jump balanced, like an Olympic diver. He felt warm tears burning behind his eyes. *It's the wind, it must be the wind.*

"Get lost, God." He muttered as he bent his knees for the leap. He kept his eyes on the radiance of the setting sun.

The sun is tucking into bed. What a moment for a tender childhood expression to creep in! He wanted to laugh and cry. *Oh God, whose favorite expression was this? Was it hers or was it his own?* He couldn't remember, but grimaced in pain at the thought of her. And then, standing on the edge of the cliff, prepared and ready to jump, Sam realized that his terrible fear of heights had miraculously disappeared. In what were to be his final moments, he had shed the shameful fear that had haunted him since his childhood. Another one that came too late!

Recklessly he leaned forward over the drop. Then he pulled back and felt the full weight of his body on his heels. *Not like this! I'm not going to fall by mistake. Wouldn't that just be typical?—blundering into death also. Nope, this time, this way will be my choice.* He leaned back a little more. He felt strangely powerful, suddenly aware of every straining muscle in his body.

"It won't end it, you know." The voice again, musing.

Sam stood quite still, his mind scrambling. *What is this? Did someone else stay behind? Was I followed?*

"Who are you?" Sam kept his eyes on the horizon in front of him as he fought to keep his balance. "Go away!" He said it with more force than he thought he could muster.

His breathing became labored. "Better still, fuck off!" Sam began to pant with anxiety. "I don't want to be saved!"

"I have no interest in saving you," said the voice. "That's what so many of you don't get. It's not possible to save another—not from himself, not from herself, nor from fate, eternal damnation, hell, or just plain idiocy, like what you're busy with."

Strangely, that hurt. The idiocy part reminded Sam of his father's words. For a fleeting moment he stood undecided. Then Sam stepped back carefully, and turned around. Gray clouds floated in, fast and low. The mountain was donning her cape of mist, veiling everything behind folds of shifting fog. Sam peered into the fading light, trying to locate the interloper.

"Who are you?" He demanded into the fog. *Are you God? A messenger? Or . . . ?*

"None of those." The deep voice had a trace of a smile in it. "No. Just a traveler, if you like, making a stopover."

Sam scanned the gray bushes, the trees, and low shrubs. *I really am hallucinating.*

"You know, you're making the wrong play." The voice was closer, somewhere in front of him. "You'll be out of the game for quite a while."

Game? "What game?" Sam felt bewildered. "Where the hell are you? I can't see you!" No reply.

"Are you saying life's a game?" Sam was suddenly furious. "Life is not a game!" he roared. "I don't know where you're stopping over from, or where you're going to, or even who the hell you are, but you haven't been around much if you think this is a game. The world is an ugly, dangerous place." He heard his heart beating in his chest. "Nobody in his right mind calls life a game!"

'Course, nobody in his right mind talks to an uninvited ghost on a mountaintop either. Suddenly, Sam needed to convince the stranger.

He needed him to understand the truth. *There is no alternative. I've got no choice!*

He needed him to know about the disappointment, until he met her. He wanted to make it clear that he had found meaning in his life through her. *But everything died, and it's my fault.* The bile rose in his throat and his stomach contracted. *It's no fucking game, mister!*

"Sam," the voice said gently. It sounded closer, though he still could not identify any shape in front of him through the fog.

"Life is exactly like a game. Life is a game with very specific rules, and if you break them, you get benched. But you are not going to be benched, Sam. You are about to leave the game altogether. Heading for the dead zone."

The Stranger

Through the rolling mist and fog, Sam recognized the outline of a man sitting against a tree a few yards away. His legs were drawn up slightly, his arms around his knees. He rested his head against the trunk of the tree. He looked relaxed.

"Oh yes, Sam," the stranger said, "this game has rules. But most never learn them. These people grow old and bitter and they die the same way—hard and full of regrets, so disillusioned—as if they had been cheated out of something." His voice dropped a little deeper. "Then there are those who play only rarely, and they are the perpetual victims who believe that the world owes them something. Most people, Sam, never learn the rhythm and never master the game. A great tragedy."

The fog lifted briefly, enough for Sam to make out a tall man, open-faced and broad-shouldered. It was difficult to tell his age. His dark, shoulder-length hair was pulled back into a neat ponytail. He was regarding Sam with a look of interest and bemusement.

"Who are you? And how do you know my name?" Sam didn't go any closer.

"I'm called Aaron. And please alert me when you're going on with your self-indulgent journey; I'll leave right away. I don't like waste." He stood up, gracefully, and leaned his shoulder against the trunk.

"What if you were never told certain things? How could your life have been different, Sam? What could you change now, if you knew the Rules of the Game?"

"What the hell do you mean?" Sam felt impatience and frustration begin to rise.

The stranger ignored his impatience. "Before you take off into nothingness, don't you want to know where you went wrong?"

Oh great! A last-minute lecture. Sam shrugged, then sighed and sat down. *What the hell. I've got a few hours to kill as long as I'm over that cliff before the first cable car comes in the morning.*

"People get confused by all the signposts to heaven."

"Excuse me, what?" Sam was surprised in spite of himself. The statement was just so outrageously eccentric.

Again, Aaron ignored the interruption. "When people begin to want to understand how to make sense of their lives, the thousands of would-be saviors out there start waving their signs that read: "This path to paradise." Of course, this is when they—the seekers—get lost." He stopped, gave a little laugh, still looking at Sam. "One of your major struggles, I might add, is exactly this. How many religions did you claim as your chosen way? How many churches gladly took your time and money? But did you ever find what you were seeking? I think not.

"If you had, you wouldn't be here, would you? Lack of meaning brought you to the mountain tonight, all that terrible emptiness is what determined death as the desperate alternative. When you lost her, there was nothing to keep you standing."

Sam felt the full weight of the mountain pressing on his chest. He could admit it. His entire life had been a struggle to please others, to meet their expectations, to make them happy. He felt the rage bubble up. *Who was this man?*

"Most humans struggle," Aaron said, softly. "They don't really understand why they struggle. They know only that they struggle, almost all the time. Struggle is what they expect, and struggle is what they get. They cannot make sense of the struggle, and they cannot make sense of their lives. That is because they were never taught the Rules of the Game. Indeed, they have no idea that there are rules.

"Many look to religion for answers. But, Sam, before you waste God's time with your problems, before you cry for help, you must learn the rules of this game. The rules are a part of the plan, and you made an agreement before you were born; you must honor that agreement. You agreed to play; that's why you are here!" Aaron gave him a wistful look. "But they had you convinced that you are help-less, sinful, and bad—that you had begun your life with a deficit of sin."

Sam remained silent, carefully watching the man in front of him. Aaron took a deep breath, and this time there was genuine amuse-ment in his voice. "God cannot help you, Sam. That is against the rules, unless you help yourself first. That's really rule number one, the helping yourself part. Interesting, isn't it? Yet we're taught that we need to be saved! But each of us is responsible for saving ourselves. A per-son must learn the rules, so he, or she, can play."

Sam leaned forward, eyeing his visitor cautiously. "Man, you are good," he said, sarcastically. "What's the price for this privileged infor-mation, by the way? I kinda hate to break the bad news to you, but I got canned today. Will you take a bad check for this cliff-edge treatise?"

Aaron smiled, and then said softly, "Sam, you looked for help. You spent the requisite hours with therapists. You tried the pharmaceutical cure. You went the holistic approach. But you never quite got there, did you? Otherwise we wouldn't be having this little chat on Table Mountain, would we? You wouldn't have been standing on the edge of that cliff."

I don't care. Take off, get lost, and go away—you're in my way. Got a date with death. Sure wish I could talk like you, tough fella! When did I ever have that conviction? When's the last time I believed in anything? Jesus, where's this coming from? "Maybe we're all waiting for a little miracle," Sam said faintly.

Aaron laughed. "A miracle? A miracle? Oh yes, that's right. A miracle is easy. Half the human race is waiting for a miracle to haul them away from their misery."

"But a miracle doesn't require any learning. So, we're back to the rescue model again!"

"Sam, it is precisely because you wait for miracles that you paralyze your independent will. When you look without your own self, not only do you exclude the possibility of what you call a miracle, but you also shift the balance of power significantly. And if you do this often enough, you will drain the vital source of belief in you and transform it into a dry clump of fears that will trip you up and haunt you for the rest of your life, and render you powerless."

Hey, a sermon on the mount! This is the stuff good stories are made of. Too bad only a dead man is listening.

"Good point," said Aaron. "Of course not much taught on that mountain is practiced. People can't seem to take in the Rules of the Game."

Great, the hallucination is reading my mind. "What are you, a motivational speaker? What do you guys go on to become? I met a few and always wondered how much they believed themselves."

Aaron didn't reply. He just watched Sam silently.

"Well, I'd like to stay and continue this conversation, friend, but I have an appointment to keep." Sam hesitated. *It's too late for a pep talk!*

But thank you very much! "And don't you have a spaceship or something to catch?"

"Sam, would you like another chance?"

Sam stood carefully. "No, thank you. Nice of you to offer, but I'll pass." He stuck his thumb over his shoulder in the direction of the cliff edge, but kept his eyes on the man in front of him. "I thought it was clear that I don't want to be saved. Nothing's changed."

"Nothing has changed," Aaron echoed. "Well, so it would appear." He smiled. "Your world is peopled with change experts, telling you where you're going wrong—thousands of mistake-specialists eager to analyze, to help the patient see how he was victimized. The patient— you—imagine that this will cure you. But you're always focused on what is wrong with your life. Herein lies the real problem—the focus on what is wrong. No wonder you're lost."

Sam felt himself leaning forward, toward Aaron. *What? I don't understand!*

"Of course you don't understand. Few do. The helping profession is big business.

But did they help you, Sam? Did you feel better after your fifty minutes, or were you even more convinced you'd been dealt a miserable hand, that you got the short end of the stick?"

Sam felt the familiar self-revulsion. "You know the answers? You can come up with some original information?" he whispered hoarsely.

"Well, let's just say I can offer a fresh perspective. The starting point, Sam, in taking control, is knowing what questions to ask. Very few ask questions, relevant questions, that is. Then of course, there is the critical issue of consistently focusing your attention in the right place. A therapist who focuses his or her attention on the problem will automatically lead the client in the same direction, back to the problem. And, through ignorance of the Rules of the Game, close the door on healing."

"What are you talking about?" Sam was exasperated. "How can a person get help if the therapist doesn't know the problem? That makes no sense at all!" He turned back to the cliff.

"Of course identifying the problem is necessary, but what follows after identification is the real key. Therapists who don't know the rules can maybe make your stay on the bench a little more bearable. But, essentially, you're out of the game." Aaron spoke quietly.

There it is again! This game bullshit.

Aaron shook his head. "So many continue to struggle through life, convinced they just don't make the cut. Like you."

Sam felt himself in familiar territory. *I can't even kill myself in peace and quiet. I get to spend my last moments feeling not good enough. Oh God, when will this end? Failure.*

"In the West, we generally treat the symptom," Aaron continued. "Why bother the patient with responsibility? Drugs can soothe all the symptoms. When you sought help in the struggle, Sam, didn't your therapist direct you to the past? Weren't you absolved of all responsibility? Weren't your parents found to be the problem? Their influence and their genes scripted your failure, yes?"

Aaron moved closer. "Your mother's shut down, your father's mistress, a bottle of Jack Daniels. Well, now you're all figured out! According to your therapy, you never had a chance. But, Sam, what if you're here to write your very own script?"

Sam said nothing. The familiar pain rose in him and he closed his eyes.

"They found your label," Aaron said emphatically. "They sold you that ticket, and you bought it because you didn't know any better. Suddenly your sad little life wasn't a mystery anymore. You got the standard treatment for having the abusive father and distant mother. The solution to your debilitating depression is the happy pill. Textbook stuff." Aaron sighed almost imperceptibly. "The world is full of poor souls like you. Ignorant of the game, they seek solace from licensed drug pushers. They thought they had you figured out, Sam, but they were dead wrong."

Sam was back in the boardroom, mute, powerless. *All my life, my whole life, I've been a shadow. Even here, even now in the darkness, I'm still the one outside.*

"Why is it like that?" Sam groaned. "Nobody chooses any of this, I'm sure of it."

"Sam," Aaron leaned heavily against the tree and looked through the mist. "What are you really sure of? Moments ago, you were sure about taking the easy way out. Moments ago, you were sure you didn't want to be saved. And since the cardinal rule is that no one can save anyone else, you can be confident that you get to make this choice."

Aaron stood eye-to-eye with Sam. "You can be sure that you will not fail this time." His eyes wandered to the emptiness behind Sam. "Good choice, the cliff," he said coolly. "Sadly, you will not soar like a bird. When you leave solid ground, your terror of heights will return like a vicious, spiteful enemy. Your final moments will be smothering panic and anguish, and you will be dead before you hit the rocks. Now there's a choice to look forward to. I'll leave you to it, then." He turned and stepped into the fog, his white shirt billowing slightly in the wind as he disappeared.

Sam stood stunned. *What . . .? All these so-called revelations, this stuff about a game he could learn to play, and then this?* He couldn't believe it! He was completely alone. Then Sam realized with dreadful certainty that he had been cheated out of his plan. He was unable to move, the paralyzing fear was back and it was very real; his teeth chattered uncontrollably. The gray clouds had dropped down low, surrounding him, and now he could see only a few feet in front of him; he was utterly disoriented. In the dense fog he no longer knew where the edge of the cliff was.

Impotent anger swept over him and he screamed silently into the wind. Then the nausea returned and he bent double to vomit the burning wave, but could only manage dry heaves. He felt the hot, shameful tears. *You spoiled it, Aaron, whoever you are! Just this once I wanted to do it my way. I finally got the courage! I stood up for once without fear. I felt powerful for the first time, and you took it all away with your game shit! You played me! Oh God, you played me!*

Sam sat down shakily, terrified that he would move in the wrong direction. He huddled with his arms around his legs, his head between his knees and sobbed as the powerlessness gripped him. He did not know if he was crying because he no longer could face the cliff on his own terms or if the overwhelming terror for the gaping abyss unnerved him so.

I don't want to go anymore! Oh my God! I can't even kill myself.

"Shit! Oh fuck! What a terrible mess!" He spat the words with anger and frustration into the blinding fog around him. But only the silence answered. Low clouds created the illusion that he had been left stranded in a lonely, white desert in the middle of the sky, lost, with not a soul around him. He knew he would be discovered in the morning. A pathetic, failed suicide.

This has to be my crowning achievement. What rules? What game? And why tell me now? It's too late! My life is over. Sam heard someone moaning. *It's me. I'm making those pitiful sounds. I can't go back and I can't move from here. Who knows these rules? Whose rules? Oh, God, I've gone mad.*

He slowly toppled over on his side and curled into the fetal position.

Life beats us all. He tasted ashes. He remembered the sea of unfamiliar faces in the street earlier when he made his way to the mountain. *Shadows, they all had shadows on them. Nobody is happy. If you have some minuscule scrap of happiness, you know you'll lose it. The jealous gods will come to claim it. They come to take it! Living is suffering.*

He muttered softly to himself. "Failure, so much failure, what is next? I don't care anymore. What a hellhole this is." He surprised himself by speaking out loud.

"It does seem like a hellhole, doesn't it, Sam?"

His body stiffened. *Not again. No more tricks.* Sam didn't open his eyes, and didn't respond. He stayed perfectly still.

"I see you did not make it to the edge, Sam." That low, gentle voice. "The fear came back, didn't it?" Inside the fog there was only silence.

"Sam, it seems to me you have a problem. You have lost whatever momentum you had to go over that cliff. Even if that were not so, your guts don't seem up to it anymore."

Why did you come back?

"Well, I noticed that you might be reconsidering. And I came back because I was meant to."

Sam opened his eyes, but remained motionless.

"Let me repeat that." Aaron's voice was calm. "I came back because we were meant to meet here on Table Mountain."

Sam felt exhausted, spent. "Aaron, are you real?" *Sweet Jesus, I sound like a lost little four-year-old.* Then he felt the hand on his shoulder; there was no mistaking it.

"Yes, I'm real. And I'm right here."

An even longer silence filled the fog. The mist swirled around them. They were locked together in an eerie vault in the sky.

I'm scared.

"I know."

Sam's voice was almost inaudible, "And I'm disoriented. I don't know which way the cliff is anymore. I can't tell in the fog."

"I can help you with that."

Sam didn't move. "Are you going to save me, Aaron?" His voice shook. "You said you didn't save . . ."

"I'm not." A strong arm encircled Sam's shoulders, lifting him to his feet. "I am not going to save you. I am going to teach you the Rules of the Game," Aaron said evenly. "After that, if you still think you need saving, you might perform that little miracle for yourself." Aaron laughed as he began moving confidently down the hill. "Come, this way. We don't have much time."

Sam followed. *He's tall . . . tall as I am.* "Aaron," Sam spoke in stride, a step behind his visitor. "You said you could teach me the Rules of the Game . . .?"

"Yes." Aaron didn't look back. "You're ready to play?"

▲   ▲   ▲

Consciousness and Awareness

*F*rom a distance, through the fog and swirling mist, the deserted restaurant with its empty tables and chairs resembled a half-built stage, missing some of its décor and all of the actors. The fog was still heavy and thick; the lady of the mountain was visibly drawing her cloak tightly about her, hiding her secrets from strangers.

Aaron and Sam approached like two ghosts from the sky striding through the rolling low clouds, eerily appearing, and then disappearing in their nebulous surroundings. Sam didn't know where they were going, or why, but was content to follow this man. He trusted Aaron even though he did not know who he was. Earlier, on the plateau, it was important to know his identity, but now he simply allowed Aaron to lead the way.

"Here?" Aaron pointed to a table in the middle of the outer dining area. "It's as good as any," he said, pulling out a chair and gesturing toward another chair opposite him.

Sam sat. Exhausted, he cupped his face in his hands and leaned forward to look at the man who had led him from the abyss. Very dark, wide-set eyes, dark brows, and a high forehead dominated Aaron's wide, oval-shaped face. His thick, black hair was caught conveniently in a neat ponytail. Deep laugh lines framed the generous mouth.

Do I know you? Who the hell do you remind me of?

Aaron looked back at him, amusement showing in his face. "Satisfied?" he asked.

Sam realized with embarrassment that he was staring at his companion.

"I am sorry. I didn't mean to stare. But I am still having a hard time believing these events." *Is this a dream? Have I lost my mind?*

"No, Sam, you're not dreaming. Quite the contrary actually—you're waking up."

Neat trick, this mind-reading thing. "Waking up? How . . .?"

"Yes, you're waking up. The journey starts here, Sam. If you do not wake up, and become conscious and aware, you cannot learn the Rules of the Game. Do you know what that means?"

Sam considered his answer. He thought about awareness and consciousness, and took his time, not wanting to disappoint the stranger with a facetious reply. "Isn't everybody alive automatically conscious and therefore aware?" he asked.

Aaron considered the question, and then he reached for another chair at an adjacent table. He dragged it around, caught it with his left foot and positioned it a distance away from him so he could put both his feet up. He locked his hands behind his head and leaned back, closing his eyes. When he began to speak his voice was soft and even.

"No, Sam, nothing could be further from the truth. It is very unfortunate, but the majority of mankind is in a state of perpetual sleep. Indeed, many people are almost comatose." He took a deep breath and continued, "I know you want to hear about the Rules of the Game, but first we must talk about Life, your predicament, and that of many others." Aaron opened his eyes briefly. "You must be patient with our discussion. Some of the information will challenge what you think you believe, but it is often necessary to be blunt to get the message across." He closed his eyes again.

"The problem is not ignorance, Sam. The problem is perception. You are not ignorant of your troubles; you are overly aware of them, and that is another problem we will come to later. It is an important rule that sidelines many. We met here on the mountain tonight, because it is time for you to learn about the game. You have the consciousness level to grasp this information." He turned his head in his hands and glanced at Sam. "Not everybody does, and that is why it is so hard to see people with the capacity for understanding, struggle so much."

He closed his eyes again. Smiling a half smile, he continued, "I know you will get it. This time, you will get it."

Sam sat forward in his chair and assumed a more comfortable position; he rested his forearms on his knees, locked his fingers lightly together, and waited.

When Aaron began to speak, Sam didn't interrupt the soft, steady flow of words.

"Earth is home to many diverse creatures, but humans suffer most because they differ greatly in their capacity to understand the complexities of their own lives. However, and this is important, complexity and opportunity to grow, interestingly, go hand in hand. Many find the complexities so overwhelming that the opportunities go completely wasted. They never get past the struggle, and therefore they learn very little. When you struggle all the time, your attention is on the struggle; there is no doubt about that. This results in circumstances that no one prefers, but everyone has to live with."

Sam thought about himself on the edge of the cliff earlier, and he wondered if this was an example of what Aaron was talking about. Aaron paused, as if to give him enough time to finish the thought, and then continued.

"Those who assume that they already know the answers to life's challenges are offended by the call to wake up, or to become conscious. They are tired of the struggle, just like all the others, but because they imagine that they have sufficient insight, they unknowingly exclude themselves from further learning. In truth, they have not seen through the folly of their relentless self-righteousness and pride, and so they keep repeating the same mistakes over and over. This they do, often with arrogance, Sam, and they don't notice, because they are asleep.

"They sleepwalk through every day, unaware of how they think the same thoughts, oblivious to the fact that what they love or hate never changes, that the very same things that angered and depressed them yesterday, still grip them today. Despite their ongoing frustrations and the fact that nothing improves significantly for them, they are convinced they've got life by the tail. And they're always congratulating each other on their expertise." A clearing had formed around them. The fog cocooned them in a world of their own. Aaron continued while Sam listened.

"Many mistake intelligence for consciousness. These are not the same.

In your world there are many highly intelligent people who do not have the capacity for understanding what we are talking about tonight. It sounds strange, but it is true. They are clever with book knowledge, but they need it all in black-on-white. They demand facts, because facts are intelligible, and they insist on proof. But, Sam, there is a very big difference between intelligence and consciousness. When investigating consciousness, intelligence is really not that important."

Sam looked up, surprised at the statement, but decided not to interrupt.

"To grasp a truth, intelligence is helpful, but an open heart and mind, seeking truth, is much more valuable. Those who pursue truth discover it has a way of knowing itself. Once found, it cannot be explained, because Truth comes from a place of feeling, and for the intellect, feelings are generally just too nebulous.

"So while some bang their hand on the table, demanding proof, those who found truth discover it keeps expanding and growing to open incredible doors for deeper understanding, leading to personal growth beyond their wildest imagination. The intellect is a trap that snares many for a lifetime, or more." Aaron smiled. "Without truth, however, the intellect becomes a hard, unyielding ceiling that limits growth and expansion of consciousness. It is what arrests awareness.

"But if intelligence is coupled with truth, the intellect begins to expand to grant insight into life's most complicated matters."

Sam said nothing. He just listened to the convincing tone of the man sitting opposite him, and took in every word. His eyes wondered over their ghostlike surroundings, and then he looked back at Aaron whose eyes were still closed. He appeared to be in a semi-dream state, but Sam sensed that he was highly alert.

"People struggle as much as they do because they fight a nameless, faceless enemy, called fate. They believe that they have the hand they're holding because some god with a warped sense of humor dealt it to them. Sam, that is not true!"

Aaron opened his eyes and looked at Sam. "Each human being creates his or her own reality. The tragedy of the human race is that few know this and it all centers on the Rules of the Game. If you know the rules, you can create the life you want, and you can really play the game. If you don't know the rules, you remain a victim for most of your life, and you struggle endlessly. You go from one frustrating experience and one disappointment to the next, always wondering when your luck is going to change, but it never does. It cannot! Not because you deserve to suffer, but because you are standing in your own way."

"What do you mean?" Sam whispered.

Aaron continued, as if Sam had not spoken. "You can never have what you believe to be out of your reach. You cannot claim anything for yourself that does not equal what you are in any given moment. The rules don't allow for that. They never have, and they never will.

"You see, Sam," Aaron didn't blink, "the Rules of the Game function all of the time. They are not concerned with status or personal preferences. They function regardless of anything in your world. The rules create cosmos in your world, not chaos. The world depends on these rules because they maintain the balance.

"But because these rules have been hidden for so long, most people break themselves against them. They try to achieve peace of mind, improve relationships, exercise more control in their lives, and move forward in life while breaking the rules. That can never happen."

Sam concentrated hard, and Aaron continued, "Why do you think is it so hard for people to change?" He didn't wait for an answer. "People find it hard to change because most are nothing but sophisticated robots, and this is the comatose state of unawareness I have mentioned. They sleepwalk through life, imagining they already know the answers. They don't notice the repetition, the struggling over and over with the same miseries. Their entire day is driven and dictated by conditioning. People like this are not truly conscious human beings," Aaron smiled crookedly, "particularly the very intelligent ones who pride themselves on their intellect. They fall hardest of all for they simply can't see the difference! To them, to be physically awake, is to be conscious.

"I repeat, nothing is further from the truth. Consciousness is not a given. We must learn how to become conscious."

"Aaron," Sam spoke softly, "I'm sure we need conditioning in our lives! How will we live if everything has to be a decision? Surely driving a car, shaving, preparing breakfast, or performing other menial tasks requires very little thinking and, therefore, calls for conditioning?"

Aaron held his gaze. "The answer is both yes and no. For some activities, learned responses work, but the majority demand awareness, and should not be conditioned under any circumstances.

"Let us look at relationships, for example. When your marriage broke down, you blamed yourself and her. That was a conditioned response."

Sam stiffened. He didn't want to talk about that.

Aaron pretended not to notice. "When your child died, you blamed God—another conditioned response." He looked away from Sam and focused on a spot far off in the mist, as if trying to pierce it with his eyes. "For most of your life, you have been a victim. Your career failed because you didn't have the confidence to fight back. You took everything personally, again a conditioned response. You felt intimidated and inferior. For that you blamed your parents, especially your father. But you blamed your mother's emotional detachment for your inability to help your wife when she needed you. You never got past the problems, or tried to change the repetitious patterns. All your responses were conditioned. There was always something, or somebody to blame. When you blame, you cannot heal. All forms of blame are conditioned responses. In the game of life, no one has the luxury of giving responsibility away. It is not an option you have. You can only give control away; lack of awareness blinds you to this truth."

Aaron sat up, resting his folded arms on the table. "Unless you learn that you create it all, you cannot play this game effectively. The world has reared a whole generation who feels entitled to just about everything; people who believe that the world owes them something, they deserve privileges, or have rights on the basis of who they are."

He leaned a little forward. "Sam, the gods pay no attention to this! No. They are interested in people who are learning to help themselves, because these people attract opportunities for advancement and growth to themselves. The 'entitled ones' fall deeper and deeper into the quagmire of their own self-perpetuating miseries, endlessly blaming others for their own limitations."

"Can these people at all be helped? It seems rather bleak to me, Aaron." There was concern in Sam's voice. "If you hadn't been here tonight, I'd be at the bottom of that cliff. Why were you there for me, and why didn't it end tonight?"

The two men sat looking at each other. Neither spoke for a while. Then Aaron smiled slowly. "Because you inadvertently activated one of the rules to work in your favor for a change. You called me to the mountain, Sam."

How? Sam stared at Aaron. "I called you? I don't remember . . ."

"The premise of the game is that you must get yourself out of any challenging situation you're in. No one can do it for you; otherwise there is no learning. I did not do it for you, you did it yourself." Aaron saw the puzzled expression on his face. "Relax," he said. "Let us take it one step at a time. You will understand; I know you will."

"How long are you staying, Aaron?"

"Tonight only, so let us begin."

Sam sat back contentedly. He felt calm for the first time this day. If life was a game, he wanted to know how to play. He wanted to know how to live.

"When I found you curled up on the edge of the cliff tonight, you asked the right questions. You asked who had the key to the game, and why you were never taught any of the rules. Well, you're not the only one in the dark. Few know the rules, and even fewer know how to apply them." Aaron looked past him again.

"A long time ago, much of what I am going to tell you was considered esoteric or hidden knowledge. It was rather exclusive. Now, think about that for a moment, Sam. Why would the Rules of the Game be hidden? If you require this knowledge to live meaningfully, why would it not be available to all?"

Sam looked at him, waiting for the answer.

"Because it is much easier to control people who are dependent. Whoever holds power must control the masses. An easy way to accomplish control over large numbers of people is to convince them that they are powerless. When people feel vulnerable, their inner sources are eroded and substituted with external dependency. When they believe that solutions lie outside of themselves, they begin the wild-goose chase around the universe. This is how all enslavement evolves. People become conditioned to rely on others to solve their problems," Aaron said. "And so they are robbed of their own selves, and they stop thinking."

"We stop thinking? Aaron, how can we stop thinking?" Sam interjected.

"Easily," Aaron said quietly. "See how quick you are to protect your cherished beliefs, the things you pride yourselves on? These are the same things that exclude you from understanding how your life comes about. Sam, when people are genuinely tired of struggling, they always seem to find the way to liberation. They stop doing what all the others are doing, and look for different, original answers.

"When you get to this point, the road opens up. You begin to recognize the repetitive patterns of the past. You begin to understand that you have a right to happiness, and you commit to find it—on your own. You begin to practice self-reliance—the principle that gets you out of the starting blocks, really fast. You begin to understand that if you ask the right questions, the appropriate answers become evident. And you develop patience. You see your life as your own responsibility. And you commit to self-investigation, and you gain insight into the unique relationship between you and your universe."

Aaron paused and looked at Sam intently. "Have you ever wondered about that? Do you think there is a reason for everything in your life? A purpose of some sort?"

Sam looked down, and remained silent for a while. The memories came flooding back. Purpose? No, he never managed to get on top of that, although he tried. There was so much on his plate. Finding life's purpose was a luxury reserved for the favored few. They had time to establish what the big picture was.

"I did." He laughed dryly. "I probably still do, but with all the troubles I've had, finding a purpose in my life seemed a daunting task. I just tried to stay alive." He felt embarrassed. "And if you hadn't shown up tonight . . ."

Aaron stared at the ground. The concrete was cold under their feet and the thin mountain air, uncomfortably chilly. "Sam, perhaps after tonight you will know your purpose. Many thousands just like you would do a lot better if they understood how they created their worlds around them. Someone has to tell them. Why not you? Just don't promise anyone flying lessons as part of the deal." He laughed softly.

Sam smiled. He didn't mind the little dig; suddenly the need was there to learn what he had missed out on.

"Self-reliance and independent thinking go hand in hand." Aaron was serious again. "You see, Sam, most people don't realize how enslaved they are. They allow others to make up their minds for them. They watch television, or read the newspapers, and imagine that what they hear or see must be true. But much of what you see and hear is nothing but propaganda. If you investigate, you will understand the truth of this statement.

"You become a truly free person when you begin to do your own thinking. That is the very first sign of freedom. It is the ability to look into matters, and make an objective decision based on your own experience and your own research. If your conclusions are wrong, the mere act of thinking for yourself strengthens the inner belief in your own capabilities, and will, without a doubt, lead you closer to the truth.

"Until you actually begin to think for yourself, you will fail to recognize patterns in your life, and remain a slave to circumstances. You will feel helpless, hard done by. These feelings push genuine control out of your reach, and make it impossible to feel positive about much in your life. Dependence on outside sources for information and assistance closes the door on true learning, relegates you to the rank of victim, and puts you on the bench."

Aaron smiled, musing a little, then continued. "People on the bench believe the universe picks on them, singles them out for punishment, and finds them every time it wants to unleash its wrath on a hapless human being. And so they struggle, without hope of any real redemption. That is when they begin praying for miracles. They want God to rescue them from the mess they have created. But God will not save you in this way. It is against the rules."

▲   ▲   ▲

Redeeming Redemption

The silence stretched as Aaron waited for Sam to say something, but he didn't. Aaron knew the challenge of overcoming conditioned beliefs was enormous.

"You think those are harsh words, Sam?" He leaned forward and said softly, "Perhaps you think it blasphemous to even mention God's role in the game? After all, everyone wants redemption, so how can God be excluded from this?"

Sam sat immobilized. Finally, he spoke. "I don't know. When you say it, it sounds right, but I think the real world will reject it outright. It is comforting for us to believe there is a savior of some kind out there, although he, she, it never showed up when I needed help most," he added ruefully.

"Who determines what the real world is, Sam? Is it your ancestors, other people, or you? If it is anyone but you, then you shape and live your life according to their experiences. Nowhere is this more prevalent than in people's spiritual experience, especially for those raised in any form of organized religion.

"The spiritual world is a busy, busy marketplace on earth," Aaron's voice had a pensive quality, "where peddlers and charlatans alike pitch their colorful tents. They squat patiently by their fires, waiting for lost souls looking for answers outside of themselves, to wander away from the city walls so they can sell them salvation." His eyes rested on Sam; there was no judgment in them.

"You became a wanderer. You visited many of these striped circus tents with their charismatic performers."

"Yes."

"Ah, they tried," he said. "They tried to win you over. A few times I thought they had succeeded. Some of them were very convincing; they had fire in their eyes and just the right lure in their voices, and they told many tales of their own redemption, and then you wanted to be redeemed also. You wanted to be one of them, feel part of a flock and belong to a greater whole.

"The need for meaning was always there, but you looked in all the wrong places. Mostly, you confused this with your childhood need to belong." Aaron sounded tired, as though he had seen what he was describing so many times, yet it still made him sad.

"Every time they signed you up and took your money, their wallets grew fatter but your need was never met—it is not hard to peddle redemption to the insecure. On some level you understood what was happening, but had no idea of how to change it. It is the emptiness of what they sold you that drove you to despair and confused you so. Thankfully, a significant part of you could not be snagged permanently."

He looked past Sam, "If you had known the Rules of the Game, you would have known better. You wouldn't have kept company with them as long as you did."

Sam sat quite still. It was like watching his life on a stage. He could clearly see the events Aaron described, the need to belong, then finding those endless religious groups, and allowing them to convince him that he had come home. How could that be if he ended up on the mountain tonight? He shook his head in slow disbelief.

Aaron stood and turned his back to Sam. He locked his hands behind his head as though he were going to stretch, but just stood there for a long time without moving. Then he dropped his hands, and looked at Sam. "Because humans do not know themselves, and thus inhabit a perpetual state of confusion, many seek salvation through organized religion. But salvation cannot be peddled, Sam. It is not for sale."

He sat down again, facing Sam. Sam noticed how dark his eyes were. In the faint light coming from the deserted restaurant, he saw the intensity burning there.

"When man's consciousness level is sufficiently elevated, he can no longer be fooled." Aaron's voice became stronger. "He might still browse around in the colorful markets or sit among the thousands in huge gatherings, watching speakers strain and sweat, demanding that lost souls choose between heaven and hell. But a conscious man doesn't buy into it anymore. An inner pull begins to draw him away from the commercialized world of cheap persuasion. He sees through the slick designer suits of television evangelists. He recognizes the fallible man hiding his own fear as he waves Holy Scriptures in the faces of hypnotized masses, cloaking himself as the chosen one."

Sam listened motionlessly, mesmerized.

"A man with a growing consciousness and awareness regards the priest who claims the power to grant absolution for past and present indiscretions, and then he turns and walks away. He knows that inside the long, flowing soutane is a mortal man at war with his own carnal desires; preaching chastity by day, while at night his body writhes and twists, protesting the denial, craving an end to the horrible charade, while struggling to hide those needs from the scrutiny of the believers. A conscious man understands that such a man does not even have the power to know himself."

Sam nodded. He understood.

"To grasp the Rules of the Game, Sam, you must step away from the quicksand of mass opinion where the blind are leading the blind in circles of garbled beliefs. Theirs is a place rife with rumors of salvation, but these are mostly stories, handed down from one generation to the next."

Sam interrupted for the first time. "Did you say belief? I thought it is all about belief, Aaron. Is that a lie?"

"No, it is not a lie. Belief is very powerful, Sam. Indeed, it is one of the rules! But belief without personal experience is meaningless. You must engage in the world, and gain all the experience possible. You cannot rely on the experiences of others. You have to discover it for yourself, for without experience, you will never own any truth. It can never be yours; it will always be empty and hollow.

"Oh, there is perpetual noise in the world, but like a marching band tuning multiple instruments, it lacks harmony. It is nothing but cacophony—a loud, tuneless babble competing for attention: 'my god, your god, this god, that one! God, Allah, Ohm, Yahweh, the All, the Nothing.' There is just no peace.

"Sam, man is what he is. But many arrogantly imagine they can force change on others. They want to convert them, bring them to their own fancy of holiness. They stubbornly insist on conformity, so everyone must reform. But a devious selfishness drives the effort to convert others. Such conversion props up the ego and promotes false power, removing the self-righteous proselytizer even further from truth. It is all self-aggrandizement, stemming from very deep insecurity. If I can convince another of my belief, then somehow mine is validated. But that is nothing but the loud voice of ego speaking.

"Society demands that people display their labels. Without these labels, our conduct is a mystery to others. They cannot buttonhole us, and that makes them uncomfortable. But a conscious man, growing in awareness and readiness, realizes with increasing certainty that he is an individual, and he wants to own it. On the deepest level, an aware man cannot be swayed. His evolving consciousness will not allow it.

"Every person must find his own cause in a lifetime, but the pace at which he grows is not dependant on the efforts of others. Our soul is not subject to the whims or convictions of those who want to save us. Our soul unfolds in its own time, just like a flower opens under a rock, in the open field, in the barren desert—when the time is right. Every person knows when the journey begins; it is unmistakable.

"Instead of looking without, we begin to look within. And life becomes a prayer as we slowly discover that what we sought so desperately out there is really inside ourselves." Aaron put a hand up to touch his heart briefly, and then continued. "We find within ourselves enough to study for a lifetime. The mystery of life begins to reveal itself, and the endless struggle is replaced with a gradual, but definite control.

"Self-observation reveals to us that negative conditioning stimulates most of our behavior, and this conditioning controls our life without our conscious consent. We learn to stand apart from our bodies and watch our behavior, and then we begin to see how the different personalities within us war and tear at each other.

"We can choose to observe these behaviors dispassionately. That is when we notice that we are not cohesive whole beings, but rather ignorant machines at the mercy of everyone who knows just which buttons to push. We also observe that if no one is around to push the buttons that normally spin us out of emotional and mental control, we do so ourselves. We have trained ourselves to run the destructive programs of worthlessness and unforgivingness, which keep us endlessly on the mouse wheel. We realize that these programs run continuously, a litany of maddening, negative self-talk in our minds. Sometimes the volume is very loud; other times, we allow ourselves a short respite.

And we get a glimpse of how thin the line between sanity and insanity really is.

"We see that, contrary to what we may pretend, we do not love ourselves. No. Instead we harbor a deep self-hatred, which is the justification for our destructive behaviors. We accept this self-abhorrence as just punishment for the many failures that lead us to feel so powerless and so worthless.

"Those who do not love themselves truly, Sam, can't play the game effectively. They fall into self-pity—a state in which they cannot be fair to themselves or to others—and they cannot appreciate the magnificent play of those who are skilled at the game, scoring points."

"Scoring points? How do you score points in the game of life?" Sam asked astonished.

Aaron looked at him for a long moment, and then replied, "There are those who gain confidence through self-examination and self-reliance, the ones who really get to know themselves. They no longer solicit the advice or good opinion of others. They choose their own path, independently, not because they are rebels, but because they understand that other people can never serve their purpose, or be their truth.

"They love others, but they don't need them. They may be despised by those who see them gaining ground, but to players of the game, it does not matter. Your performance is unaffected when those who are benched, dislike you. It counts for nothing, for they are powerless to influence you."

Sam got up and walked a few steps into the fog, breathing deeply. This night was turning into a much greater challenge than he had envisaged. Instead of finding oblivion, he was being called back to life, and he didn't want to miss the call. He wanted to know where he went wrong and why he had struggled so much. Most of all, he wanted to learn how to live. He turned and looked at Aaron. He didn't know where to start.

So it is a game, a game with rules, which it seemed, only a few privileged people knew. He had not really heard any of it yet. No, Aaron was building up to it. Sam had always considered himself open-minded, but now he felt unsure. He noticed how he shied away from the stranger's suggestions that perhaps he, Sam, could learn a few things.

Aaron looked at the figure standing a few feet away from him and answered the unspoken question calmly. "The hardest part of learning something new is letting go of the archived behavior patterns. You have to let go of those cherished, preconceived ideas that you confuse with truth."

Sam didn't turn around.

"Your mind must be open so you can perceive the negative conditioning, and acknowledge how it has trapped you in repetitive behavior patterns. These patterns negate thinking.

"Most people don't see this; they don't want to hear it. They believe they have all the knowledge they need to play the game, to live successfully." Aaron folded his arms and laughed softly. "But then they buy lottery tickets because, really, they just want to end the pain hidden behind all the bravado and show. They delude themselves into imagining that there are shortcuts in this world. There are no shortcuts, Sam, not one."

"Aaron," Sam turned to look at the man standing a short distance away from him. "I admit that much of what you have said so far makes sense. I might even have heard some of it in the past. I can't say for sure. However, with all due respect, this sounds a bit like Philosophy 101—the kind of drivel impressionable students lap up because they believe that their mission is to reform the world." Sam looked down at his shoes. "They have not lived much, and as you said, no truth ever becomes ours without experience. But there is a problem. Countless numbers of people truly wish to find a way to cope better with their lives. From time to time, I was among those people. That's why the self-help industry is flourishing. But in my experience, few of us make progress. It is not that people aren't interested in improvement; they are, and I believe I was too. It is just so hard to follow through, to transform it from theory to practice in daily living!"

Sam moved closer. His hands were in his pockets, his arms pushed in against his body; the cold mountain air was getting to him. "I still don't know what tomorrow holds for me, but I am willing to deal with that later."

He stood a few feet away from the stranger and looked him in the eye. "I am glad that I did not make it over that cliff tonight, and for now, I am happy about our meeting." He smiled crookedly. "Even though you are a mystery to me, I am willing to let go of that also, at least for the moment." He laughed. "Really, Aaron, judging from some of the material I have read, your presence has a dozen different explanations. Who knows? Perhaps Captain Jean-Luc has a search party out looking for you and the Enterprise is about to swoop down and beam you up!"

Aaron smiled, but said nothing.

Sam became serious again. "You see, Aaron, one of my biggest struggles has been to marry theory to experience, to make it real. In the end, everything was just crazy mind games, volumes of learned information without any real substance because I did not know how to practice it." He closed his eyes for a moment. "Tonight is an experience I might not be able to speak about without being ridiculed." He paused and thought about his next statement, then said deliberately, "But I am willing to risk that if what you claim to know will change my life. However, in my view few people evolve. Oh, they try. Some read books; some go to seminars; and some huddle together at weekend retreats. Others attend ashrams in faraway places, hoping some of that holy shine will rub off—but it never does. The veneer of fake change wears off very quickly. Is change really possible? Why is it so hard? Why, Aaron?"

Aaron studied the man in front of him. He had not interrupted the flow of his thoughts, for doubt and fear follow the human being like faithful shadows. Even in darkness, when no one else can find you, the shadows know, and they always come. Unless Sam learned the rules, tomorrow he might doubt the meeting here on the mountain ever happened, or fear that he had imagined it. Sam's deepest fear, of course, was that he was being duped again, that their conversation would turn out to be more useless information, more philosophical drivel.

Aaron liked that expression; it accurately described the mental meanderings typical of the blind leading the blind. They talk endlessly, but they have no real experience; you hear only the hollow echoes of their words as they try to convince others.

"Let's sit," Aaron said, pointing to the chairs again.

When they were facing each other across the table, he continued. "I mentioned earlier that you create your whole life, and every human being does this, consciously or unconsciously. You call your life into existence, you make it happen, and you do so by virtue of who you are."

He looked intently at Sam. "Yes, the correct word is 'create.' Try to lose the Old Testament connotation of the word for a moment." He continued, "You create your own world and your own life, with a force only those who know the rules comprehend.

"Without knowledge of this force, you're out of the game. You will never get what you want because you will be breaking the rules all the time. Everything will be working at cross-purposes in your life. You'll be frustrated and depressed and unable to make any real changes. I am describing the plight of the majority of humankind," he said, with compassion in his voice, "for this force holds the secret of creation."

Sam returned his gaze, puzzling over the force and its secret.

What could it be? Miracles or magic perhaps? Even special gifts?

None of this felt right.

"What is the secret of creation, Aaron? I really have to know what it is." He could hardly contain himself.

Aaron remained silent, observing Sam's mind thrashing around, attempting to navigate with the same confusion and frustration that marked the race. Then he answered quietly, "Vibration is the answer, Sam. The secret of creation is vibration."

▲　　▲　　▲

Energy and Vibrations

*I*t was dark and very cold outside at the tables where they were sitting. Through the windows of the restaurant, Sam could see neon signs flickering on and off, beckoning customers who would not show up until the cable cars transported them up the side of the magnificent mountain the next day, laughing and excited. Outside the big glass doors on the verandah, the tired red eye of a Coke machine stared at him without blinking.

He didn't look at Aaron. He struggled to recall some of the theories he had read in the past. He couldn't remember anything about vibration. "Vibration? That's the secret?"

He felt disappointed. He had expected a big revelation, or an obvious answer that he had overlooked—the gold key that could unlock all the doors and solve all his problems. He had expected, wanted so much more! He didn't know how to react. He didn't want to embarrass the man here with him, but he really felt the urge to laugh. This just couldn't be it!

Aaron observed the play of emotions across Sam's face: The disappointment, the veiled indignation, and then the hidden embarrassment. He didn't answer Sam's question, but kept perfectly still and waited.

"Aaron!" Sam jumped up, unable to hide his disappointment any longer. "What happened to all the talk about the Rules of the Game? rules, games, and secrets! Perhaps the tooth fairy will show up shortly to point me to the castle she built with the teeth she harvested from my childhood!" He began to breathe heavily. "Please, let us be real. Make this worth my while, I beg you . . ." His voice trailed off.

"You want us to be real, Sam?" Aaron asked evenly. "Now what reality would that be?" Aaron got up, walked around the table and stood beside Sam. He gazed into the fog, still heavy and thick around them.

"Is it what you know as reality, or is it what you want to be real for you?"

Sam looked up at him, beseechingly. Aaron kept his eyes steadily ahead of him, unwavering. "Which one, Sam?" he enquired softly.

"I don't know," he was suddenly uncertain. "I don't know if I understand what you mean by—"

"Do you know what reality is, Sam?" He did not wait for a reply. "I think not. Come," he said, "let us walk a little. It is getting colder, so let's keep moving."

Sam fell into step beside him and buried his hands in his pockets as they began to walk in a great circle around the parameters of the building.

"The principle that underscores the entire game is to understand that everything you see—everything you call reality—is essentially an expression of energy. In the busy material world, this is the principle, so many don't see or understand. Lacking this insight automatically obscures the rules. Ultimately it results in people's elimination from the game; they are benched. They don't know that what you call real, must obey the energy laws of the universe. They don't know this, Sam, because they can't see it.

"They only know that they don't have what they want, and they bitterly envy those who seem to have it all. They don't understand that it is the envy they feel, that brings into their lives more things to feel envious about. Those who sit on the bench attract to them all that they hate, all that makes them miserable.

"In other words, what they feel strongest about, they literally call to themselves. This is the quagmire I mentioned before. When people are in trouble, they focus on that trouble. They think about it, despair, and brood about it. The stronger they feel about it, the deeper they sink into everything they so desperately want to avoid. To understand reality, Sam, you must be able to perceive beyond your physical body. Do you imagine what you see with your naked eye is everything that is real?" He turned to look at Sam. "It is not, but we will discuss this in more detail later. Let me start at the beginning. And the beginning is not only how you think but also what you think about."

Walking silently beside Aaron, Sam suddenly remembered something Aaron had said earlier that night, on the plateau. "You said that I called you to the mountain tonight. I don't understand. I don't remember calling anyone."

Aaron slowed his pace, and then stood still. "Yes," he said. "Outwardly you wanted to end your life, but your strongest desire was to understand how you got to that point. Your journey in this life, from the beginning, has been one of self-discovery. All the different religions, organizations, and groups that you joined, however briefly, expressed your inner drive to know and understand your life circumstances. In the cable car you thought that only a miracle could save you, remember?"

Sam's thoughts went back to earlier that day. He remembered the rotating cable car and the nausea that threatened to overwhelm him. He remembered that there was nowhere to look without seeing, feeling the heights, and then he had closed his eyes and prayed to be somewhere else. His terror of heights paralyzed him. He had called on all his strength not to surrender to his cramping muscles. Oh God! This terrible mountain, how could he get away? Who could help him? Only a miracle could save him.

Standing in the cold mountain air, Sam remembered. "That's when I called you?"

Aaron nodded his head. "The strongest desire always wins. It is the emotion behind the desire that creates the circumstance you want. When you desire something intensely, and your attention is on what you want, that emotion is very powerful. Your desire to live was much stronger than the desire to kill yourself." Aaron paused. "So I showed up."

He smiled. "I showed up because this was your real desire, and because, in your heart, you truly believe in miracles."

Sam observed the man on the mountain path with him. He could hear, and feel every word but struggled with the meaning, the full implication it held for him.

Aaron continued, "Sam, thoughts are real. They are expressions of energy, and energy by nature cannot be destroyed. It can change, it can be transformed, but energy cannot be destroyed. As expressions of energy, thoughts have a magnetic quality about them. They either attract or repel. They have a frequency.

"Similar thoughts attract each other, and dissimilar thoughts repel each other. If you want to understand the Rules of the Game, then you must understand the most basic fundamental: All is energy.

"Throughout our lives, we process millions and millions of different thoughts, from the very dark to the absolutely ridiculous, and, quite often," he said with his quirky smile, "the sublime. Over the years we learn to model our thinking and behavior according to our parents' or other role models' example.

"Your parental example was self-destructive. However, your own experiences are also part of the mix. So too is your faint memory of how you came into being, manifested in your search for truth, your evolving beliefs, and above all, your hope and desire to find that truth one day. The sum total of all of these parts equals your energy indentification or energy fingerprint, if you prefer. Put another way, your energy ID is a personal frequency at which you function most of the time, thus it determines what is possible or impossible in your life."

"So there is such a thing as fate? You are what you are because of parents, upbringing, and background?"

"Some see life that way, Sam, but they're benched. Fate gladly gathers victims in its name, convincing them of its power, and then leads them into a downward spiral of helplessness and powerlessness.

"I tell you that if you raise your consciousness and increase your awareness, you can overcome anything. You alone set the limits of what is possible. But in the game of life, those on the bench don't see their infinite potential because they constantly focus their attention on their predicaments and failures, their losses, and the unfairness of life.

"Sam, life is not about the hand you are dealt, but surely about how you play the game. Your thoughts create your world. There is no better way to say it. Thoughts are magnetic, and similar thoughts resonate together, according to the Law of Resonance. Thoughts, by nature of their frequency or vibration, attract one another. You can verify this law with any musician. Musicians know from experience that when they have two pianos in the same room, and strum middle C on one, the same note on the other piano will begin to vibrate in harmony with the vibrations of the first. And that law lets you into the game, or hauls you off the field.

"Perhaps you know this principle as the Law of Attraction. Thoughts that resonate on similar frequencies are naturally attracted to each other; they are drawn to each other. This law, not fate, or luck determines all. It determines what you have in your life, whom you associate with and what circumstances you ultimately choose to make your life in.

"And this law takes its cue from you! You are the beacon, the station that sends out the original thought vibration! The law itself is impersonal and has no preferences. It has no capacity for caring or for making judgments. It does not speak any human language, nor does it care in which language you think and speak.

"Its language is energy and energy only. It reads your frequency, and your frequency is generated by your own thoughts. You create your own world with your thoughts. So your enthusiastic and loving thoughts, by law, attract similar thoughts into your life. If you think negative thoughts, these become the basis of what you attract into your life. For, as you will see later on, thoughts result in experiences.

"People live in their circumstances and associate with specific other people, because of who they are, because of their energy fingerprint. They attract what they have into their lives because everything vibrates in harmony, be it good or bad. You could say that their energy fingerprints are similar, so they 'read' each other."

They had walked in a very wide circle and were back at the tables. Sam was very quiet. He thought he understood some of what Aaron was saying, but he needed to ask many questions; he wasn't sure that this night would have enough hours to illuminate the struggles of a lifetime. He felt the cold, but somehow it didn't matter.

"Why don't we know these things? If thoughts are that important, why are we not taught, as children, to be mindful of our thoughts?"

"Who would have taught you that, Sam?" Aaron asked quietly. "Your parents didn't know, nor did their parents or their parents. You cannot teach what you don't know. For many hundreds of years this had been exclusive knowledge, but it no longer is. Significant traces of similar teachings have appeared in the myths and folklore of all cultures and religions, but people fail to pay attention. This information is not religious in any way, and no denomination can claim ownership of it. This knowledge is universal and timeless."

He smiled at Sam. "Have you heard the saying, 'as you think, so you are'?" He didn't need an answer; he saw it on Sam's face. "Or, 'birds of a feather flock together'?" He gave a little laugh, "It means nothing other than what I shared with you about energy ID.

"If you carefully observe life around you, you will see evidence of this principle everywhere; you have to be virtually blind to miss it! The carefree child playing in the garden—who is still part of the dream world—sees and attracts invisible friends to come and play and share her joy. Joy and happiness attract more joy and even greater happiness, because of the compounding effect. But when negative conditioning takes hold and she is taught to be real—to disregard her imagination—sadly, her little friends must find another place to play. They cannot find the child anymore, for her frequency has changed to one who no longer expects mysteries to be part of her life.

"In every walk of life this principle attracts people to each other, or repels people from them. Those who gain insight and understanding grow together. Others submit to being victims. The abused and abuser are both victims, both drawn to each other by feelings of deep unworthiness. It can be no other way.

"The priest, the imam, the religious leader who stands in front of his congregation is assured of their following. They come together because they think similarly, their frequencies are complementary, and they support each other because they are convinced of their mutual spiritual intent.

"The man who finds his pleasure with the prostitute cannot deny that he is any different from her. The financial exchange recognizes the same basic need, sex without connection. It matters not that he is important, a figure of status, maintaining a magnificent . His essential self inevitably takes him where his energy resonates, and determines his fate."

Sam listened quietly, for he sensed that understanding how energy functioned could lead him to understanding the rest of the rules.

"Remember those family gatherings that you hated so much when you were a child?"

"Yes, of course."

"What did you not like about going there?" Though the question sounded simple enough, Sam thought it somehow significant. He thought back in earnest, to remember why he disliked those family occasions so intensely.

He recalled the shrill voices, and the noise, the running, screaming children. How difficult it was to connect with anyone in particular. Then he knew. He knew why he didn't want to go there, why he always sought excuses for not going.

He hated their behavior and the things they talked about! Someone was always complaining about a physical pain of mysterious origin. Then conversation would deteriorate into a miserable sharing of all physical things gone wrong in the past, or still to come. Relatives would initiate a bizarre competition to upstage each other in pain and suffering. The skilled hypochondriacs among them couldn't be outdone. Nobody could fully understand the extent of their sufferings, and no one was allowed to forget that. It remained a dark mystery to the medical profession and to them, but they never tired of telling tales of their wretchedness.

How he hated that! He always felt out of place. As the day wore on, they would divide into factions. While the sick ones relentlessly recounted stories about their ill health, others who couldn't compete on the disabled list would disengage, to shout through political or religious discussions. Their ignorance was matched only by their loud voices, clamoring for supremacy. The spectacle of eyes and veins bulging in the effort they made to win would terrify him. He would end up sitting in a corner, waiting for the day to draw to an end, anxiously looking for an excuse to make his exit. His family was insufferable! He always left feeling drained and tired, but he never knew why.

"Do you now understand?" Aaron inquired. Sam no longer wondered about how Aaron knew his thoughts, although he hoped for an explanation before the night was over.

"I never understood how they could talk about the same things over and over, or why they never tired of complaining," Sam said, with a nervous laugh.

"Misery loves company," Aaron smiled. "You'll never run out of people to talk to if you want to complain. Do you know why you felt so drained afterwards?"

"Not really."

"They stole your energy from you. They sucked you dry, not purposely, of course, but inadvertently. When you have a higher level of consciousness, your energy is more refined and others register you as different, or strange. And if you are among a group that functions at a much lower level, you cannot draw them up to your level. No, you get dragged down to theirs, where your energy is transformed into negativity—anxiety, for example."

Aaron was deadly serious, Sam could see that; but nonetheless, he felt uncomfortable. "Aaron, this is a bit like *Star Wars* stuff. I mean, can this really be true?"

Aaron didn't respond to that question. "So, when you become aware of what is really happening, you have a responsibility to stay away from such groups. Or, at least, you have to learn how to protect yourself." He looked at Sam, sensing the question he wanted to ask. "You'll know how when the night is over." Then he continued, "Most people never learn the rules; they blunder through life wishing for things to get better, hoping for improvement. But it never happens.

"Instead of finding the cause of the problem, they give up hope and fall into patterns of self-pity and self-destruction that are very hard to overcome." Again, he smiled crookedly. "With some exceptions here and there, that accurately sums up the human race.

"So they begin to play the blame game, but blaming others puts you firmly on the road to ignorance. Blame always excludes the possibility for understanding and healing. It paralyzes the conscious mind and disables objective thinking. Blame declares the problem is outside of you, and a mind that believes this, blinds itself to inner illumination.

"It cannot find higher ground and automatically shuts off forgiveness to itself and others. The game, Sam, goes on regardless of what you know or don't know. No special concessions are made for anyone. It does not matter if you know any of the rules, or if you believe in them, or if you do not.

"Part of learning how to play the game is discovering that there are rules, and then learning them, so you can move forward—become good at the game. The possibilities after this are endless."

Aaron eyed his companion wistfully, and then shifted into a more comfortable position. "The secrets of conscious living are locked up in the laws that govern this and all the other worlds. Few discover them, for they are too busy with the material world and its problems, and they are too enamored of facts.

"Often when they come into contact with this information, they arrogantly dismiss it as pseudoscience, or new age nonsense." His eyes softened. "This they say despite the fact that they have not found the answers to their most pressing problems, and notwithstanding the reality of these laws and principles having been around since the beginning of time. They stubbornly maintain that the ethereal cannot be proven, and what they cannot measure with their limited minds, they refuse to accept or investigate.

Ah, you see, fact always wants to have a contest with truth! Black on white!

"Prove it! That is the demand. Their ignorance comes from two sources: the first is their refusal to investigate the rules, because they self-righteously assume they already know what they need to know; the second is their assumption that science can explain all that is necessary to know.

"Yet one of their most revered scientists gave them the clue they all choose to overlook. Einstein glimpsed the special mysteries of the universe, for he said, 'The intuitive mind is a sacred gift and the rational mind is a faithful servant.' His real insight was into humankind's state of mind when he added, 'We have created a society that honors the servant and has forgotten the gift.'

"Thus, it is intuition, the gift, and that inner knowing, that opens the doors for those who learn the Rules of the Game. They become tired of the drug prescriptions, the stale advice of those who are as ignorant as they, and begin to look within to find truth.

"They give intuition a chance, and a magnificent inner journey of self-discovery begins, directed by objective self-observation. And they never regret it, for truth abides fully within. This principle of self-discovery, this inner journey, is clearly articulated through all time and everywhere, mandated in all advanced cultures and religions, there for all to see."

Sam sat listening quietly, fascinated with Aaron's calm and focused delivery. He thought about the principle Aaron spoke of. "What do you mean? I don't think I have ever come across it."

"You think not?"

"No, I don't think so . . ."

"Why, it is 'Know thyself.'" Aaron said quietly.

Sam sat motionless. He remembered some of the poems and essays that he had read, many of which touched him deeply, but the adage always remained theory—someone else's elevated thought. He had never practiced it; he didn't know how to do it!

He had no idea of how to get to know himself, how to benefit from the instruction to improve his life, and he was sure that many others struggled with similar difficulties.

What was missing? Why was it so hard? He looked at Aaron who sat waiting.

"You know now, don't you Sam?"

"The Rules of the Game? That's the missing piece of the puzzle?" Sam whispered.

Aaron smiled. "The Rules of the Game. Yes. The set of principles, the laws that make it possible for you to learn new things and, through practice, implement in your daily life. The same set of principles that can show you where you make mistakes, why you suffer, and how to change that. The keys to personal power in taking back the control you lost. Without this information, Sam, life remains a mystery to most. They swing like a pendulum from ecstasy and bliss to depression and darkness, and then they look for a savior to come by and rescue them. They search high and low to find ways of extricating themselves from the mental and emotional maze they're lost in. But they never really find it.

"Many imagine that religion holds the answer, like you did, but when they leave their spiritual gatherings, and look into their hearts, when they are alone, they know that their demons have not left them. They are still plagued by the very same fears they try to run from every day. The same terrible desires burn in their hearts. They still covet their neighbors' wives or crave material things beyond their reach, and incapable of facing the person in the mirror, their only alternative is to ascribe their deceit to the failings of human nature, failings that God should understand and forgive them for. They imagine themselves to be in a position to bargain with a God they try to placate on a Sunday and forsake on a Monday."

The two men faced each other in the cold mountain air. Both seemed oblivious to the weather. The fog was heavy and thick around them, but they were focused on the conversation. Sam felt that a part of him was wide open, a part of himself he was not familiar with.

"These people do not grasp the importance of energy, how they sculpt their lives with their very thoughts. Everyone is constantly moment to moment, busy creating his or her own life, either consciously or unconsciously, with their minds. The only language that the universe understands is energy. It does not interpret or choose. It has no preferences and does not 'know' you other than to recognize your energy fingerprint, or ID, through frequency. It picks up your vibration or energy ID and accordingly attracts circumstances, to bring events and people in your life that function on a similar level as you, to demonstrate to you what you are thinking. Consequently, negativity is not a luxury humans can afford!"

Sam looked at Aaron in dismay. "That is very harsh, Aaron. It's impossible not to be negative from time to time. After all, we're human."

Aaron laughed as he shook his head. "What happens to your creations while you're busy being negative? Whose responsibility is your life then? No, my friend, you cannot afford careless or directed negativity; they are not building blocks. You cannot eliminate them all at once, nor can you completely banish negativity over your lifetime, but you can make a start, by becoming aware.

"This world is nothing other than energy in motion. It is dynamic and moves forward all the time. You must develop the ability to look past your physical body, and see, feel that there is more to you than meets the eye."

"I think I have always believed that, Aaron." Sam said indignantly.

I'm not that ignorant! "But it's impossible to prove. It's more an article of faith than anything else."

"Have you believed this, Sam? If you had an inkling that all you see, is not all there is, where does that fit into the greater scheme of things and how does it benefit you to know this? Do you mean you have an eternal quality then, hidden from the mortal eye?"

Sam looked away, uncomfortable. "Well, I hope so. I don't actually know it. I am not sure of the heaven-and-hell thing anymore, but I think there is a continuation of some kind after death. It just seems the most logical explanation. Otherwise, how can it just end like this? What would the purpose of that be, especially for those who were born with absolutely no opportunity to advance and grow?"

"Good thinking! Sam, if you are eternal after death you must have been so before birth. Think about it. Eternity is not a quality you can casually and at will award to anything at a given time—that would be completely illogical. If you are at all eternal after death, you must have been so before birth. There can be no other alternative." Aaron eyed his companion with great interest.

"You are an expression of energy, and energy by nature, is indestructible. Everything in your world is energy, and before you can understand God, or the complications of your own life, you must understand that all is energy. Understand that you use this force, this energy that you cannot see, but generate at your own given frequency as determined by your thoughts, to create your world around you. To gain true insight, you must first know yourself. Without self-knowledge, nothing, not even God, can save you!"

Sam stared at him incredulously, but Aaron went on, "All your problems exist because you create them. They reflect your energy ID. And they are there to help you learn. Sam, if you went over that cliff tonight, you would have reached a dead end. But if you are capable of seeing what I am talking about, you can get back in the game." He smiled broadly, joy showing in all the laugh lines. "It is all energy, Sam! It is nothing but the expression of energy cleverly disguised as your problems, challenges, and fears. The fingerprints of the inner you are all over your life, and they show up as both your difficulties and triumphs. They signify both your ignorance and your insight."

Aaron looked him straight in the eye. "It is impossible to lie, Sam, another rule of the game. This rule mandates that your inner world always reflects your outer world. You can pretend as much as you want, but the keen observer will always know the difference."

"There is only one way to effect permanent change, and that is to take a good look inside. Know thyself, and everything will change."

▲　　▲　　▲

You Are
Your World

"Why don't we hike a little bit? We still have much to talk about, and I don't want to overwhelm you, so let's give this a little time to sink in." Aaron turned without waiting for agreement, and walked away into the mist.

Sam followed, glad of the distraction. He felt weighed down as he tried to make sense of the talk about energy, and of Aaron's assertion that it was impossible to lie. He didn't understand it, but wanted to believe it. *Maybe I'm just gullible.*

"A gullible person," said Aaron, expertly finding his way in the dark, "is ignorant of the true facts. When you don't know enough, another can easily convince you. But that is not our business tonight, Sam."

"Where are we going?" Sam asked.

"We'll go east for now, in the direction of Devil's Peak." Aaron laughed, picking his way through the low brush and proteas growing wild on the mountain. "And appropriately so!"

"Why?"

"I want to talk to you about the rule responsible for the demise of many marriages and relationships, just the same way many of you blame the devil for all that goes wrong. And ignorance of this rule results in the endless frustrations of daily life.

If the average person were more tuned into his world he would see the logic and recognize the rhythm of it. But most are not, and therefore they suffer. They suffer because they try to push against nature."

"I don't understand," Sam said, following closely behind. "How do we do that?"

Aaron suddenly stopped, and his companion almost collided with him. "You know what a chameleon is?"

"Of course."

"Don't you think it ingenious how that little fellow can accustom itself to the environment to disguise and protect itself? It has an almost miraculous way of corresponding to its surroundings so it can hide its presence!"

On the narrow path they were face to face, staring at each other in the darkness.

"I've never thought of it, but I suppose it is quite unusual." Sam didn't know where the conversation was leading. Chameleons? It was all so strange.

"Humans can do something a thousand times more miraculous," Aaron said emphatically. He looked at Sam, as if waiting for him to catch on. In the ensuing silence, Aaron turned to continue his easy stride along the path. Sam followed.

"Humans can change their environment to suit them. It is also one of the laws."

"What is it called?"

"The Law of Correspondence. Just as water always finds its level, your Energy ID or fingerprint is all over your life, and finds its level. It is unavoidable."

"What does this mean?"

"Your outer world is an expression of your inner world. Because energy finds its level or frequency internally, your reality reflects your deepest thoughts, values, and beliefs. These are externalized in your life circumstances."

Sam grabbed Aaron's shoulder from behind. "No!"

"No?" Aaron stopped and turned to face him.

"How can that be? What is, simply is. There is nothing we can do about it! If what you say were true, that would be miraculous, but I don't see how."

Aaron laughed. "If you think of this as a miracle, then miracles happen in your world every day! This is not a matter of miracles, Sam. It is nothing but the simple distribution of energy as determined by your thoughts! Everything that you are on the inside appears on the outside. There is a continuous movement and balancing of the internal and external scales going on. Your outer world reflects your inner level or frequency, as generated by your thoughts. Life is nothing but energy in motion. That is why you cannot lie! Your external reality always reflects what you are on the inside. It is a natural law at work."

"What did you mean when you said humans push against nature?"

"Humans insist that external circumstances change first, as if they can set conditions for others! They think they want to play the game, but on their terms. They look at their problems and insist the problems disappear before they can be happy again. Countless people go through life unhappy, feeling hard done by, because someone else needs improvement. Many people assume that if only another person could see the error of his or her ways, and change, they themselves could be happy again. What nonsense. It cannot happen!

"We draw to us everything that vibrates in harmony with our internal landscape.

Everything that resonates to our personal frequency—all energy that recognizes our internal energy ID—comes to us. We call these circumstances and this reality to us, because of who we are. To therefore insist that someone changes before you can be happy goes against the nature of things. You have to change first; it starts with you."

Sam drew away.

"Sam, you cannot expect to compromise this rule, for it operates in no other way. Your inner and outer worlds must correspond to each other, and they always do. This is the Law of Correspondence. Your outer world continuously transforms itself to reflect your innermost thoughts and beliefs. If these change, according to the immutable Law of Correspondence, you will begin to attract the circumstances and people into your life that correspond to your altered beliefs. This is the necessary balance I spoke of."

Sam stood on the path in the cold mountain air, trying to make meaning of Aaron's words. He thought of her again, and the child. He remembered her bitter accusation that she was forced to mourn the death of the child alone because of his emotional remoteness. He remembered the pain in her face, and how he recoiled from her need for his consolation. Squeezing his eyes shut, he shook his head, tried to block the memory. But her anguished face remained.

He wondered how their lives could have been different had he been more aware. Perhaps he could have saved the relationship. But he couldn't bear to think of it, not now. His loss still hurt too much. The loss had brought him to the mountain tonight.

He dismissed the thought with determination, opened his eyes, and turned to Aaron. "How do I do that, Aaron? The ability to change oneself sounds like a miracle to me."

God, why could he not let go of her?

"You're thinking of her."

"Please, not tonight." Sam looked away.

"No, it is not a miracle, Sam," Aaron said, recognizing his distress. "But it does require discipline. If you change your thoughts, your inner world will begin to transform. When you do that, your circumstances will change accordingly." He looked at Sam, "It does so automatically, without effort or strain. If you don't like what is in your external world and you want it to change or improve on it, then you now know the rule. You have to change first, by changing the way you think about it.

"Everything in your life molds itself after the energy print you hold internally, shaped by the way you think. Until you learn how to do this, not even God can help you."

Sam smiled. "The Christians will have your hide for that statement."

"Sam, this law is evident everywhere. Let me give you a universal example. What do people worry about all the time? Lack of money, not abundance of it! 'I don't have enough money' is a common complaint, yes? This lack consumes them, fills their minds with the direst consequences such as loss of status, insufficient material things, embarrassment, and bill collectors knocking on their door. They suffer sleepless nights with terrible fears of being destitute. They hate not having money! And they need to have more. And they so desperately want it.

"People envy those who appear to have enough money, and their envy reinforces their sense of deprivation and lack. They curse God for not taking care of them. Meanwhile, they spend their energy plotting, pleading, and scheming to get more of what they truly believe is far beyond their reach. Impossible! They must sit on the bench.

"Tragically, their agony over the lack they experience is all in vain. It is a useless and pathetic display of ignorance of the Rules of the Game. They frustrate themselves endlessly, because they push with all their might against their own nature. They want to be wealthy and live in splendor, while their energy print declares bankruptcy! How can money come to them? It cannot.

"Unconsciously, they take themselves out of the game. They cannot see the genuine purpose of their lives which is to investigate and learn the secrets of their world. And they remain victims for a very long time.

"Others, tired of the struggle, begin to wake up and look around. They read and try to determine how they can get back in the game. They discover that others before them have pursued the same quest, and found some answers. They learn wealth is a belief. And that it is the mind that brings abundance, no matter what you believe or have been told. They also discover that they will never have abundance while they crave it, for craving of any kind is confirmation of lack.

"They gain insight into their own problems, and understand how impossible it is to have abundance, when the mind perceives only lack. They resolve to change the way they think, and only then real change begins.

"These people have accomplished a much subtler and more complex trick than the chameleon. They made their environments change according to who they have become.

Now, wouldn't you call that a miracle, Sam?" Aaron didn't wait for a response.

"When people are willing to relinquish their stranglehold on victimhood, they're ready to get back in the game."

All was quiet. It seemed as if the night held its breath in anticipation.

Then Sam spoke, "What about relationships, Aaron? Money is one thing, but relationships are much more complex. There are two minds searching here."

"Your mind is filled with her, and the child. But yes, if it is a Law or a Rule, Sam, there are no exceptions. The rules apply universally to wealth, health, and your relationships—to every facet of your life."

As he turned and resumed walking, Aaron spoke over his shoulder, "All is included. You are responsible for creating your own life and the circumstances you live in. Where your mind goes, your body and your world follow."

He walked faster, as if determined to arrive somewhere. "This is not arcane knowledge, Sam. We express our awareness of this rule in ordinary conversations regularly. For example, 'a person must be trusted before he becomes trustworthy'; 'if you want a friend, be one'; 'if you want understanding, be a good listener.' So people know this rule, but do not apply it, demonstrating that it's easier to parrot pretty phrases than do the work themselves. Most people intend for the other party to comply." He grinned his crooked grin. "It is humankind's greatest weakness. People are so gifted, with so much potential, but they are always waiting for a miracle, because they do not truly know themselves.

"They search for answers somewhere out there in the world. They await the miraculous to come and find them! They fail to look within and see the miracle of what they already have, and what wonders wait to be accomplished."

They walked in silence, with just the occasional stone rolling away or dry stick cracking under their shoes; their breath made white clouds in the cold night air.

"Aaron, if conscious awareness determines our level of understanding and our ability to assume responsibility, then not everybody is at a point where they can grasp this information?"

"Correct. Hence the distinction between consciousness and intelligence we spoke of earlier. Clearly a certain readiness is implied, Sam. No one questions or conquers anything that is beyond his consciousness level.

"Fact is, most people chafe against what they see as their lot in life, but never ask questions! No," he insisted in response to the protest in Sam's face, "they don't ask the right questions, the hard questions that can lead them to understanding. They don't ask questions that will stretch their minds. Questioning what you don't understand with an open mind is mandatory to achieving greater insights and pertinent self-knowledge—to really know thyself.

"People pay lip service to the great Law of Cause and Effect. However, they neither know nor truly want to know the significance of this rule. They suffer, but attribute their suffering to 'God's will.' They complain about their needs, but wait to be rescued. When there is no rescue, it is God's will again. Everything seemingly inexplicable, or not to their liking is ascribed to God's will, or the devil's mischief.

"Most people are quick to claim the credit when all seems fine, but when their 'luck' turns, they scramble around looking for the scoundrel who did them in. When they cannot find a person, or a system, or an institution to blame, they assume Job's job. They look up at the sky and cry, 'Why me, Lord? Have I not suffered enough?' The question alone confirms their victim status. The cry externalizes their thinking and shows how they see themselves and their world. It's a declaration of their helplessness, and therefore excludes any significant possibility for self-discovery and understanding.

"Everything unwelcome is done to them. So while they warm the bench, others who respect and know the rules, play the game.

"The ignorant are oblivious to their choices. They don't see this because their awareness does not allow for clarity. Their sole, conditioned response is to find explanations outside of themselves. Nothing changes for them, because they themselves have locked and bolted the door that leads to understanding. They zealously guard the door within that only they can open."

"I recognize the importance and truth of what you are saying, yet I don't know if I have ever known how to make it mine, or how to put it into practice," Sam said.

"You have not practiced it at all," Aaron responded, softly. "But you can learn. When you understand how you create your life around you, you can change or eliminate that which no longer suits you. You alone shape the life you want, but this ability is not a gift bestowed upon you. This is your single most important purpose, your greatest responsibility! You can have what you desire in life because you can exercise control over your mind and your thoughts!"

He says it's possible to control my mind. I don't know how to do that. My mind drives me crazy. There's a demon somewhere in my head that never lets up. Even when I want to stop thinking, my mind has a mind of its own! "My mind ignores my will and runs a nonstop negative commentary. How do I control a mind such as this?"

"It is a difficult concept to grasp, Sam. We assume that we exercise free will, but we lose sight of the conditioning that undermines that freedom. We assume free will is our birthright, and that all our thinking is our own, but we are oblivious of the vice grip that conditioning holds over us. We make no allowances for how this mechanizes many of our responses, and makes our thoughts and behaviors robotic.

"Exercising control is tremendously difficult, but any person serious enough about change can learn how to do it. To accomplish this, you must first become an independent thinker."

"I am an independent thinker."

"So you think, Sam. But think about this, then. Remember earlier tonight when we spoke of consciousness and awareness? We agreed that these shape perception, correct?"

Sam nodded.

"Perception facilitates the understanding of independent thought. Those who learn the meaning of independent thought also understand freedom. The source of their understanding is their own experience, not the borrowed views of TV anchors, political or religious leaders, texts, or any words of those who claim to know the truth.

"Now these liberated people no longer go along with the crowd, no matter how strong the pull. They reclaim their free will because they know that they can choose, and they know how to choose."

Sam's jaw was set. "We all have free will. It is what sets us apart from the animal kingdom."

Aaron nodded slowly. "You're sure then, Sam? You're sure that you have free will?"

"Well, don't I? Don't we all?"

"Think about it, Sam. Free will is not a given. You earn it by learning that you can choose. When you don't make conscious choices about your behavior and responses, you are nothing but a highly sophisticated machine, programmed, as many are, for self-destruction."

"This is all very confusing. I want to know more of this information, especially the mind-control aspect you talked about, but now you're onto free will. I always thought it was a given, but you're telling me it's something to be earned! Truthfully, everything you are trying to teach me seems very complicated right now! And what about cause and effect? You mentioned it but did not elaborate. Is that a Rule or a Law, or is it the same thing?"

"Come; let us go to the viewing deck nearby." Aaron said. "It is not far."

"We won't be able to see anything. The fog is too dense." Sam said stubbornly.

"Please walk with me." Aaron started walking. Almost absently, he added, "There are only two categories of humans, you know, regardless of race, religion, or culture." They were approaching the viewing deck. Sam could barely see through the patches of fog lifting here and there.

"And you're going to tell me what they are," he countered, when the silence began to stretch.

"Oh, yes." Again Aaron's small, crooked smile appeared. They had stepped onto the concrete platform of the viewing deck. The fog swirled thickly around them. Aaron seemed ghostlike.

Sam waited, eyeing his companion curiously.

Aaron turned to look at him. "In this world there are people, and then there are 'sheeple.' And only one of these is authentic in everything they do."

▲   ▲   ▲

The Devil's Thing

"You've never been here?" Aaron included the deck overlooking the east side of the mountain in his expanse gesture.

"Mountains and high places are not exactly my thing."

"Ah yes. But you know the locals call the fog 'the tablecloth of Table Mountain.' Are you familiar with the legend of how the fog came to the mountain?—the contest between Van Hunks and the devil?" Aaron asked, leaning against the waist-high stonewall.

"Yes. Van Hunks, an eighteenth-century pirate retired from his life at sea to sit smoking his pipe on the mountain. Then the devil happened along and challenged him to a smoking contest." Sam tried to remember who had first told him this story. He had no trouble remembering the terror and awe the mountain had always evoked in him.

He continued, "Legend has it that Van Hunks won the contest, but then the devil revealed himself to the pirate and they both vanished in a puff of smoke. The smoke became the cloth that spills over the mountain, when the southeastern wind blows in the summer months."

Why are we speaking of folklore? I have only this night to clear the fog in my own mind. "Sheeple and people, isn't that rather blunt? And why are we talking about a legend, when I need to know about the rules?" He sat down on a low bench, looking up at Aaron. "How does this help me?"

Aaron stared into the fog that still obscured their view of Devil's Peak. "Many myths in your world became recognized truths through popular acceptance. The Van Hunks story is obvious and none give it serious credibility, but when it comes to conduct of life, people play the most unrewarding game in the world. It is called 'Follow the Follower.' It is the sheeple's game, but it is the devil's trap because it keeps them oblivious to truth.

"Sheeple blindly follow where they are led. They trust the ones in the front, not because they believe those in the lead know better, but because they are too lazy or disinterested to find the way themselves. It is easier to let others do the work, or to accept the status quo.

"They choose to ignore the fact that when they let others do the work, they must live with others' mistakes and misdirection. Very little of what they so vigorously defend, do they actually own. They copy or repeat from other sources. Their opinions are essentially borrowed from equally uninformed friends or especially sources of mass communication."

"You're saying these people don't think for themselves. I find that hard to believe!"

"Of course they think, Sam. When you meet them they can be brilliant in their chosen vocations. It is not theory they cannot master, for they generally love facts. In spirit, however, they are vacant, their thoughts are not authentic. They do not examine all the alternatives. They prefer to research sources that validate their own beliefs. And all their research is framed by their preconceptions of what is true and right."

"I don't understand. Give me an example of what you're talking about."

"Organized religion is an obvious one," Aaron said. "Let us look at the results of the righteous, those with the better god, or the one true god. For as long as we can remember, they have killed others invoking the name of their god. They believe they are right, their leaders have told them so, and so they go to war.

"They worship a loving god, a supreme being of divine judgment. But they judge on the life and death of the innocent. They decree the will of their god, with their own limited understanding, pretending to know the will of a divine being of whom they have no personal experience!

"They justify their actions by referencing their own 'holy' books, or their only too human leaders. If you seek a logical rationale for their behaviors, you seek in vain. They need to be right; objectivity and truth are sacrificed to justify their need."

"You are saying that we cannot rely on our leaders?"

"And why rely on anyone, Sam? Why would you want to? Are they not also mortal?

"Why not rely on yourself, and learn to make up your own mind? Then you could listen to others and decide from your own experience if their cause is worthy of your support. Many leaders exist by default because people do not know how to govern themselves. They happily give this responsibility away. Beliefs of the masses that their leaders are better informed are a myth; an example of what they accept, without questioning. It is no more credible than Van Hunks' contest with the devil."

Sam remembered his own church upbringing. He thought of his parents' regular Sunday attendance. His father always came home to the whiskey bottle while his mother withered away in loneliness. *Why did they keep going there? If nothing ever changed for them, why did they persist?*

"Because it became a habit." Aaron's voice was very calm. "They did it because it was expected of them. Habits are very hard to break; habits create both winners and failures. Your parents sat on the fence all their lives. They didn't believe in the god they worshiped on Sundays, but they didn't disbelieve either. They were simply keeping their options open.

"Religion was a convenience for them, a conditioned response they learned from their parents. Your parents had something in common with the fanatics. A fanatic holds a puny faith, and their faith was also very small. Their faith never became real; they wore it like a garment, easily discarded once the service ended.

"Fanatics are what they are because they lack substance and balance. And when you lack these, all that empty space has to be filled with loud words or sometimes, terrible deeds. It becomes a desperate act to prove you are real."

"Are we going to talk about God tonight, Aaron?" Sam was uncomfortable. *It's difficult enough here on the mountain learning the Rules of the Game.*

Aaron smiled at him.

"Aaron?"

"You don't want to talk about God because you don't understand that energy. Your mind is layered with conflicting beliefs and half-truths, but most of all you cower before a force whose existence you're not convinced of but whose wrath you fear. You confuse religion and spirituality because the former lies without and the latter within, but you have no real experience of either. This heightens your uncertainty, so you would rather avoid the subject altogether. You will discover in time that avoiding this energy, this force you call God, is impossible. But for now, we will not talk about God—at least not in the way that you can imagine.

"Before we can talk about God, you must learn the Rules of the

Game, and learn how to help yourself. You must take control of your own thoughts, your emotions, and ultimately your life. Until you learn how to do this, you will be pleading for help from a being who cannot hear you. Not because it doesn't care or isn't listening. But because you are tuned into the wrong frequency!"

"What?" Sam stared at him, incredulous of the statement.

Aaron ignored Sam's indignation. "Raise your level of awareness and consciousness, and you can know God. Not as in a dream, or a wish, or a figment of your imagination, but real knowledge because you will experience Him from an inner source. You'll know from experience. Come, look!" Aaron gestured to a spot next to him.

Sam got up to stand beside him. In front of them the fog opened up as if someone had gently lifted a curtain to one side. There was a sheer drop beneath them, but Sam felt safe. He watched with wonder as the clouds and fog opened just enough for them to glimpse Devil's Peak.

"So that's where they sat and smoked."

"Yes." Aaron sighed contentedly. "Sam, the sheeple of this world are not unintelligent, don't ever make that mistake. On the surface, they appear to function quite normally. They go about their lives like everyone else but their model—their paradigm of the world—is very different from that of one who is awake and aware."

Sam fixed his eyes in the distance. "You mean how they see the world?"

"Oh, yes. But remember, we each see the world as we are. That is what determines our paradigm or model, and that is also what we in time create to be our world. The world molds itself after you!"

"You've said that before. I still find that so hard to believe! I was raised to think the world is a given, that we just have to learn how to deal with it. I was convinced that I was helpless to change anything in my life. The odds were stacked against me! Or so I thought."

"Sadly, that is how many think, and they never learn that they can change that thought. They feel hard done by, for they were not the chosen, and they bitterly envy those who are."

Aaron threw his hands in the air. "They just accept their circumstances! They whine, but they just accept it! They don't ask questions, they don't investigate anything, for their conditioning and their belief in limitation is too strong. They cry that they want to be happy, but they never learn that happiness is a choice! You have to make that choice. It cannot choose you; you have to choose it!

"They sleepwalk through life, always looking for a savior to show up, waiting for divine intervention, but they wait a very long time. Real help never comes because you cry for it. It comes because you're ready for it, and being ready is an internal state, easily detected in your energy ID."

"That's why you came tonight?"

"You have been ready for a long time."

"I thought tonight would be the end. I didn't know how to carry on anymore. So many things had gone wrong and I just couldn't see my way out."

"You begin to understand, don't you? Your happiness belongs to you. It is your own responsibility. It depends on no one and nothing else. The most important principle of the game is that you create your own life. You play the game equal to who you essentially are. The people you meet, the circumstances you're in, all match your personal energy ID."

"Why couldn't I see this before?" Sam groaned.

"You had a very different paradigm of the world. Your model was of a world fundamentally unfair, a place where only the lucky or privileged triumphed. You were neither lucky nor privileged. Your parents were average. They struggled with a failed relationship and not enough money all their lives. You were raised in a firm belief that marriage is difficult and making and holding onto money even harder. You envied others.

"And of course, envy pushes affluence out of reach. You learned a consciousness of lack, and the immutable Law of Energy adjusted. If your energy fingerprint screams lack, then you attract circumstances that demonstrate to you just how little you have. So much of your focus was on your deficiencies that you had to experience them. Belief and experience are partners. Your consciousness always matches your environment and your experience; it is law."

"But that rule renders us helpless! If we are born into circumstances . . ."

"Your argument is not reasonable, Sam. Many people—born in the most dismal of circumstances—rise to become independent thinkers and great achievers. Ultimately, it depends on the individual and his model of life."

"So one's model can change, given the right impetus. I mean, life happens to us and influences the way we think and feel. We become conditioned to think a particular way, and it is very hard to break free. But it is possible to change; it must be, otherwise nothing would be worth the effort." Sam was uncertain.

"Life does not happen to you. The person in control happens to life. What matters is your model or paradigm—how you see the world. Sam, you asked questions from a young age. You suspected that things could be different, although you had no idea how to make that happen. Even though your discontent did not bring you any closer to the answers, you kept investigating, hoping to stumble upon an answer, or a clue. That was your saving grace."

"But I ended up here on the mountain!" Sam said, exasperated. "I have lost everything—my wife, our child, my job, my self-esteem! Right now, Aaron, I believe I am learning, but tomorrow . . . I'm not sure that I have any idea of how it will play out. I dread tomorrow."

"You dread it?"

"Aaron, come on, talk is easy. Of course I dread it! I am hoping with all my heart that what I am learning here tonight will allow me to change. My thoughts create my world. OK, that seems logical. But how do I make the learning work for me? How do I tune my thoughts to the right frequency you've been talking about?" Sam hunched up his shoulders and whispered, "I begin to see what you mean about people behaving like robots, how destructive and dangerous conditioning is. You are saying that we function most of our lives on autopilot. We react daily with very little conscious planning or thinking. You're saying that we are mostly sleepwalking . . ."

"Correct, Sam. The sheeple syndrome we spoke of, or the devil's thing if you like, that keeps you asleep," Aaron said softly.

"But must I then become a rebel and swim upstream while everybody else swims the other way?" Sam frowned.

Aaron studied his face briefly, then looked away, his voice even and controlled.

"No, Sam, not a rebel. Rebels hardly ever achieve their goals, because of where they place their focus, which is another important rule of the game we'll get to. All rivers eventually flow down to the ocean; there is no point in swimming upstream. But you must find your own way amid all the noise in the world. You have to find your emotional and mental balance and feel that you are making your own choices and decisions.

"The ability to stay balanced while the crowd buys into mass hysteria is a sign of one who is discarding the shackles of conditioned behavior, and becoming truly free. The stimulus is the same for all, but the response of a free person is different because he chooses it."

"The sheeple concept has nothing to do with intelligence then, but with consciousness." Sam spoke more confidently. "And we're mostly unaware of how our lives are the result of conditioning. Unless we learn how to become more conscious and aware, we will make very little real progress in life. We will continue to make the same mistakes over and over again.

"You're saying it is the ability to choose our responses that sets us free. When the stimulus comes, regardless of what it is, we always have the opportunity to choose how we will respond. This is the essence of free will! We exercise our free will only when we break away from conditioning and begin to make choices, Aaron." Sam continued hesitantly, "This means I could have handled the meeting in the boardroom today very differently ..."

Aaron waited.

"And it means that both she and I . . ." Sam stopped.

"You have both made mistakes. One is no guiltier than the other."

"But she blames me!" Sam felt the emotion rising.

"And you blamed her. Both were conditioned responses. Both felt the pain too severely to take responsibility. You chose to look outside of yourselves for answers, which meant that you would never heal. It may feel natural, but that way you never learn. You begin to repeat experiences, not all the same, but similar, wherein you are always the victim. And you respond in the same old ways."

"She had a nervous breakdown. How can I ignore that?" Sam asked shakily.

"Nervous breakdowns come from looking too much outside, and not enough inside."

"How can that be?" He blurted, frustrated. "She blamed herself for the death of the child!"

"Self-blame is not objective or instructive; rather it is a way of perpetuating the problem. And neither is blame an effort to really look inside, it is a hunt to find a culprit, and the culprit always gets caught, because you cannot hide from yourself! It is the worst kind of punishment there is because it cannot stop unless the person sees the futility of his or her own actions. It is self-defeating and futile. More important is the truth that it excludes forgiveness on all levels.

"It claims responsibility for all, not from a perspective of understanding, but from the victim stance of having been chosen to suffer, which results in another terrible form of blame, called remorse. And remorse is a dangerous emotion, for it is a refusal to forgive oneself. Her refusal to forgive herself put her in the hospital. Your refusal to forgive yourself brought you to the mountain. The remorse you both embraced led you into a downward spiral of self-pity. Neither of you has played the game well for a long time."

"This is a rule in the game?"

"What do you think? Can you perform well if most of your plays are conditioned? Can you really claim responsibility for your life, when you follow programmed behavior? Is this conscious living?"

"Many would disagree with you about responsibility. Most people would argue that they are responsible."

"Perhaps, but not in the way I refer to, Sam. I speak of the ability to be response able. I speak of the ability to respond to life on a moment-to-moment basis, through choice and preference, not conditioning and not emotion. And living your life this way, Sam, is a whole different matter. It is what establishes the ability to master your destiny."

▲　▲　▲

Responsibility and Choices

*L*ow clouds had moved in, hiding Devil's Peak from view. "Come, let us keep moving," said Aaron. "There are not many places to go if we want to stay on the flat surface of the mountain. But about two kilometers of pathways will take us to twelve different viewing decks. Let us see how many of her secrets the mountain will reveal if we visit these." Again, Aaron started walking without waiting for a response. Again, Sam followed.

"This concept of responsibility, can we talk about it? I've always considered myself a responsible person, but now I am not so sure. Responsible people pay their bills on time, generally obey the law—like not running red lights, and just do what is expected of them, you know . . . behave." Sam hesitated. "Right?"

"Well, Sam, that's how most people see it, anyway." Aaron navigated his way gracefully around some silver trees. "You know," he said, touching one gently, "these beauties are indigenous to the mountain, but very rare in the rest of the world." He didn't wait for Sam to comment on the trees, "It is the ability to be response able that distinguishes those who stay and play the game."

Response able means, able to respond? Then I guess I've been mostly response feeble. "I simply did what my parents did. I followed their example—like a sheeple.

"Some of my most negative responses like withdrawing into silence, I learned from my mother. She used silence as a way to punish my father. For me, it was a coping strategy, when I didn't want to deal with something, some unpleasantness. My wife, called it my 'mute mode.' She said I never let her know where the 'sound button' was. I never left clues to explain."

They had reached the deck overlooking the magnificent harbor of Cape Town. Dark, low-lying clouds obscured their view. "We'll wait. There'll be an opening soon enough," said Aaron firmly, scanning his eyes over the cloud mass. Then he turned to look at Sam, a delighted grin on his face.

"You're absolutely correct in relating this to the example your parents set in your childhood, but let us go back to the beginning of this discussion. You are making progress. When you understand this concept of how to be response able, you hold the keys to freedom in your hand, and you are ready to learn the rest of the rules."

Aaron sat down on a bench and leaned back, resting his head against the stone barrier behind them. He stretched his long legs out in front of him, seemingly relaxed.

"The responsibility we are talking about, Sam, is not optional for anyone. Why don't you sit?" he said evenly. "This conversation may take some time."

Sam nodded, and then sat. *How odd. We both like to stretch our legs when we're sitting.* "Why don't we have an option?"

"People cannot give responsibility away. They can only give control away! No matter what they tell themselves, they always keep every ounce of the responsibility.

"To be response able means the capacity, the ability to choose your responses, and this is the starting point of control. Those with a relatively high level of consciousness and awareness, learn this concept very quickly, and then practice it daily. The difference is unmistakable, because regardless of the stimulus, you always have the power to decide, or choose how you will respond. The more aware you are, the higher your level of conscious response and control. Notice, I did not say 'reaction.' The word is 'response.'"

Aaron sat up. "Most people react, they don't respond. Reaction is knee-jerk behavior—thoughtless and mostly out of control. It is a mindless thing. Reaction is emotionally charged and externalized, and, ultimately, can hurt only you. Can you see that?"

Sam didn't answer the question directly. "Do you mean the conditioning aspect? We are so conditioned to react in a particular way that we lose control over our thinking faculty and become like robots?"

Aaron grinned, obviously enjoying himself. "Well said! If you do not choose your response, you lose control over everything else that follows, because you essentially set up a pattern that you unconsciously have to duplicate."

Sam stared at him, frowning. Aaron waited briefly and then continued. "Let me give you an example. This morning when you were driving into work, remember noticing the car in your rearview mirror speeding behind you?"

"Of course, he alarmed me! I was in the fast lane and already driving over the speed limit. That idiot was driving very dangerously."

"Ah, and what did you do?"

"Well, I knew he was going to try to pass me and force his way in front of me and the car ahead. Drivers like him endanger everyone on the road!" Sam felt the indignation rising again as he remembered how upset he had been.

"So you sped up to close the gap just enough so that he could not get in?"

"Right." Sam's indignation disappeared. He felt a slow flush rising. "Well, I wanted to make sure that he could not get in because he would just go ahead and do it to everybody on the road." Sam looked away.

"So you were watching him, monitoring his movements, anticipating when he would make his move?"

"Um, yes."

"And how did you feel while this was happening?"

"Aaron, I was upset!" Sam protested. "Oh come on! Who wouldn't lose his cool? The guy was an idiot!"

"So your responsibility is to educate all the idiots on the road? Who put you in charge of this?"

"Listen, someone has to teach people like him a lesson," Sam said, not believing the words himself.

"Well, this person did not get the lesson," Aaron said, smiling sweetly at Sam. "Actually, it seems this 'idiot thing' you speak of is contagious. When he did manage to squeeze his way into the fast lane, you tailgated him all the way into the city, jockeying for your leading position."

Sam, grateful for the darkness hiding his embarrassment, said nothing.

"You did not choose your response this morning, Sam. Instead, you reacted. You reacted as millions of people do daily, in vehicles on the road and in other areas of their lives, including their relationships. Every day, millions of people communicate mechanically, putting no real thought, if any, into their responses. What upset them yesterday enrages them all over again today. They learn nothing about themselves or about the people whom they think they love. Their behavior cannot change because they repeat the same, stale, automatic reactions of yesterday, and the day before, and the day before that—ad infinitum.

"Today the stimulus was the speeding car. Conditioning caused you to put your foot on the gas pedal, and from that moment on you lost control. A complete stranger—an idiot in your words—then controlled your feelings and behavior. I want you to think about that."

Sam sat motionless, staring at his feet. Then he slowly shook his head in disbelief. "You're right. I lost control. No. I gave control to that guy. Oh my God!"

"That's just the beginning," Aaron continued. "Your freeway experience set the tone for the rest of the day. You arrived at work anxious and angry. You knew today was going to be an important day for you and yet, you took no precautions to ensure that you would arrive in the best possible state of mind. On the contrary, by the time you entered that boardroom, your victim mentality was already in place, and you were spoiling for a fight."

"That's not fair." Sam felt himself withdrawing.

"Why is it not fair?" Aaron asked softly, ignoring the symptoms of withdrawal.

"You know." Sam's voice was inaudible.

"It is best you say it." Aaron persisted.

Sam struggled against the familiar invocation—shut down . . .close off. "I went to the hospital yesterday," he could hear himself panting with the exertion. He closed his eyes, and leaned his head against the wall directly behind him.

"She wouldn't see me." His lips barely moved. "She never wants to see me, ever again." Sam felt the hot tears burning behind his eyes and put his head in his hands.

"That was the end for me. When I left the hospital, I didn't care about anything. I kept thinking 'What the hell happened here? How had we come to this?' I kept thinking about the beginning, of how we met. Oh God, how special she was! I had dreamed her into reality and now it was over, it was all over. How could it be over? I dreamed the dream and she became real. And dead is dead, right?"

Aaron was silent.

"Dead dream, dead baby, dead job, dead-to-rights failure. Everything is very much over, I would say." Sam gave a shuddering sigh.

"Your little girl died of sudden infant death syndrome," Aaron's voice was beside him, quiet and calm. "You could not have done anything to save her. She was only three weeks old."

"That day was a nightmare," Sam continued, unable now or unwilling to stop. "Poor Karla. It had been such a difficult birth, and she was so tired. I felt she wasn't coping well, and I was no help. I was caught up with work. We were losing a big account and it was easier to deal with that than . . ." Sam inhaled deeply. "No. We hadn't been truly communicating well before the baby was born. I was depressed, without knowing why, and she said I had shut her out by refusing to talk or express my feelings.

"I had called home that day to check how she was doing. She said the child had been crying all morning and had just gone to sleep. She was tired and teary, and the baby had been fussing all morning. When the baby finally went to sleep, Karla wanted to rest too—while she could. I wanted her to get better, so that I could get better; I was so impatient with her frailty. How selfish of me." He sounded exhausted.

"When the conversation ended, I felt empty and resentful. She fell asleep beside the child and only woke up hours later when I came home. The baby was on the bed beside her, dead." Sam covered his face with his hands as he remembered Karla's utter disbelief. She had grabbed the baby to her, and desperately tried mouth-to-mouth resuscitation. He remembered the horror of the colorless and immobile doll face, the tiny rosebud mouth, now blue-tinged. The baby's eyes were closed as if in dreamless sleep. Karla had only given up when she realized that the skin under her hands had gone cold.

He had stood paralyzed in the doorway, looking at them. But he had turned his face away at the pain on her face. She had screamed for him and cried in despair, but in that moment he could neither move nor help. He had stood there as if in a dream, powerless, yet certain that the baby was dead, and that nothing could be done. He had never seen a dead person, and he was astonished at how nobody needs a formal introduction to the cold hand of death.

There had been no time to get to know the baby. There were no happy memories. Karla had struggled through a difficult pregnancy, had been confined to bed for the final trimester, incapable of enjoying carrying the child, and then, finally, it was born—premature. It came silently into the world, seemingly unwilling to make any effort itself, and was delivered with forceps without as much as a whimper. It looked dead at birth. He should have known then.

"Aaron," Sam asked emotionlessly, "how can God allow this?"

"You were childhood sweethearts," Aaron responded solemnly.

"Soul mates. We were soul mates." Sam felt distracted. He began to wonder anew what could have been done differently. How could it all have been avoided?

"Soul mate is a widely overused and misunderstood term, Sam. I do know, however, that you are convinced Karla was taken from your rib."

"I don't want to talk about this anymore."

"No? Yet you have no peace, you have not dealt with this situation at all."

"No."

"At the risk of pointing out both the painful and the obvious, events occur in our lives over which we have no control. Your baby's death is an example. Later you will gain insight into this." Their eyes briefly met.

"Meanwhile, remember that lack of awareness is the main reason for repeating hurtful behavior toward others, and yourself. People prefer to run away from their problems, which is why they are never understood, nor resolved.

"You see, Sam, there is no getting away from it. You do make your world happen around you and that cannot be changed. No one is exempt from any of the rules. If you do not deal with a problem, you deal with the consequences of ignoring it.

"Unconscious behavior makes you run in circles and obscures the truth from you. The truth is that you have the freedom to make choices. If you don't know you can choose your behavior, you justify your reactions as 'human' and 'normal' and this excludes the possibility of any real learning.

"You fall into a downward spiral of negative thinking, even into depression, and you begin to expect the negative. When you expect the negative, you have very little control over your life. It becomes a self-defeating, blind battle in which any small improvement is always temporary because it lacks self-examination and self-study, creating the illusion that the improvement came from outside of you. But it is only self-examination and self-observation that lead to greater levels of control and liberation."

Aaron looked Sam directly in the eye. "In the absence of this hard work, humans cast their eyes skyward, and pray for a divine intervention. 'God help me! Make all the pain, the frustration, and the depression go away! I am weak, and cannot do this for myself. I don't have the skills or talents. You have abandoned me to fight a battle that I am not equipped for and cannot win! Why can't other people see the error of their ways? My life would be so much less complicated if others understood how they hurt me.'"

"That is very harsh," Sam said edgily, "especially coming from you."

"Ah, you think so? Would you prefer I commiserate with you, and discuss the raw deal you got?" He stood up abruptly and walked toward the lookout point. Lights were beginning to show dimly through the cloud cover.

"You did not call me for that. You have had a surfeit of temporary solutions that did not work. You know they did not work, because you continued to repeat the same mistakes, both of you, alone and together. Yes, you love her, but that love guarantees nothing. Your marriage could easily become yet another sad statistic. The child is dead, and nothing can change that. But what if what you see as a life-destroying calamity," he turned to look at Sam, and stepped closer to him. "What if you were to see this calamity as an opportunity for growth and understanding?"

"You're suggesting that perception is easy, that everyone should know how to do this."

"No, it is not easy, and no, not everyone can accomplish this transformation. They need to be awake. Only aware people can be response able and take control by learning from their experiences."

"Not if she doesn't."

Aaron's eyes rested on him for a long moment. Then he leaned his arms on the wall in front of him and looked toward the opening in the clouds. Far away the dark sea was sprinkled with many lighted ships waiting their turn to sail into the harbor early the next morning.

He spoke softly. "Yes, that is the problem, Sam, your insisting that forgiveness is conditional. You are saying that you will change if the other person changes, preferably first. This attitude demonstrates your lack of understanding of how to do unto another as you would have another do unto you. These phrases are intended for the improvement of the other person. You do not know how to find the plank in your own eye before you look for the speck in your brother's eye.

"You see your progress as halted by the decisions and behaviors of others. It is this perception that keeps you benched. It is this projection unto others that means you are hardly ever in control of your own life. But emotional well-being and balance is as much a choice as happiness is, Sam," Aaron said evenly.

"How do I get out of the downward spiral you spoke of?" Now Sam too looked out at the horizon. "Being here with you on the mountain makes it sound easy, but I know it is not. Earlier today I could not see any solutions; I felt so overwhelmed with my failures and inadequacies. I know many others feel the same kind of vulnerability, and probably find other equally inappropriate ways to deal with their crises. We all seem to struggle so hard, but get nowhere."

The cloud cover began to lift further and the magnificent sight of the entire harbor came into full view. A dazzling display of lights traced its way along the shoreline and up toward the foot of the mountain. Moving vehicles appeared like tiny fireflies, scurrying busily in all directions, even at this hour.

"You have to become conscious first, a condition many human beings claim to have, but do not. Those who argue hardest for their awareness are often the deepest asleep. When you are aware you understand that it is possible to have something different from what you presently have. You create your own world, and you embrace responsibility for your own happiness.

"But you are powerless if you wait for miracles or think only some of your life is your responsibility, and the rest is up to God.

"The human being is a creature of habit. Positive habits lead to success after success, just as negative habits lead to failures. But you can learn new habits that will lead to better choices, and result in preferred outcomes. To learn a new habit, your mind has to be open. And you begin with honest self-scrutiny. You have to commit to practicing the new habit, and then you have to do it. Otherwise, you might as well not bother. Self-help seminars and books cannot work if the lessons are not practiced. Most devotees never truly implement the content, because they don't understand the Law of

Energy. It takes commitment and focus, Sam, and both are hard work.

"It starts with how you think and what you think. Everything begins in your thoughts. Without gaining insight into your thought processes, and without acknowledging your responsibility for creating your life, nothing will really help. You need control, and you also need willpower. Indeed, without willpower, control is not possible."

"How so?"

"Your will is not a power among others, Sam. Your will is neither the first nor the last of the powers. It is all the power there is."

▲   ▲   ▲

Give Me
the Controls

*W*hile Aaron gazed on the distant, dark ocean, Sam looked inward. *How will I remember this? How will I realize this break-through that can transform my life?*

"Write a book," Aaron responded, smiling now at Sam. "And why not?" he said, at the surprised dismay in Sam's face. "Don't ask who will read your book. If your intention is to help others, your audience will find you. Besides, you need a career change!"

"I never thought of myself as an author."

"It is about the work, Sam, not the title. The value is in the service, and all people recognize this. When you focus your attention on the service, the rest follows automatically."

"Aaron, let's go back to control. You have spoken of the importance of control, but control is not easy for me."

"It is not easy for most people because they don't understand that there is a law that controls control! Let me elaborate. You are familiar with motivational talks and positive affirmations?"

"They are intended to be beneficial!" Sam interrupted.

"Right. For those who follow through and put them into practice."

Aaron folded his arms and looked at Sam, "But you have to know how to do it. If you don't know how to use an affirmation or implement positive new ideas, you begin to lose your belief in these tools. After a while they just don't work anymore, because you have become conditioned to negative results and you no longer expect them to work. Many people have similar experiences with religion. They have no personal experience of what they say they believe, and so think they can put God up against a wall."

"You say the strangest things—what do you mean?" Sam shook his head in disbelief.

"People are prepared to have faith, but first they want proof. They will believe in God, as soon as God proves that he or she exists. Impossible! We cannot negotiate the terms of our beliefs, because we create what we believe! Therefore demanding proof that God exists, is resolute denial of that force, a clear disbelief, and eliminates any possibility of proof. There is that, and then in the name of religion, people practice yet another piece of self-deception."

"What is that?" Sam asked quietly.

"People trick themselves into believing that they trust God, when really it is their own egos they worship. And it is easy to tell when you're dealing with one of these people because they are often arrogant and have foul tempers. It's not usually a pleasant experience."

"Do you know God, Aaron?"

"Do you, Sam?"

"I thought I did," Sam said wistfully. He looked at Aaron. "I assumed that you had a direct connection to God—that you were a messenger of some kind—but now I just don't know. Who are you?"

"Who are you, Sam?" He looked at Sam kindly. "Before you can know who anyone else is, you have to know who you are. Without knowing that first, you are easily swayed and influenced by others, for to know who you are, is the foundation knowledge that everyone needs."

"How, then, can I know myself?"

"By knowing what you value, because you are what you value. Look to where your thoughts are most of your day, for then you will know what you value. It all is really simple, Sam, but humans make it very complicated for themselves. Authentic spirituality is not fact based, and you won't find it in a book. It is a widening, an opening of the consciousness. Strangely enough, the more you learn about yourself, the more you will learn about God also. It is what prepares the way.

"But this is not a matter the 'religious' want to discuss. They imagine that committing philosophical ideas or religious dogma to memory automatically changes basic nature. They imagine it will lead them to God." Aaron smiled, he seemed lost in thought. "God doesn't come to us through learning, that power reveals itself through insight, perception, and feeling."

Sam smiled too. "Tell me about the Law of Control, then."

"The Law of Control dictates that you are in control of any part of your life to the degree that you feel positive about that part. The converse is equally true. You are out of control, and to the exact degree, of that which you feel negative about. Would you say most people are positive, feel good, and are in charge of their lives?"

"Of course not!"

"Would it be accurate to say that many people battle with negative thoughts and negative expectations all day long?"

"Unquestionably, yes."

"According to the law, then, they would not be in control most of the time?"

"Where are we going with this, Aaron? Why do we have so little control?"

"People lack control because they are tyrannized by anxiety, a most out-of-control way of thinking! It is the most lethal enemy you have, for anxiety comes from how you think, Sam. It is generated from an internal source and it gains momentum if not checked."

"My approach to the meeting today, and my reaction in the board-room . . ." Sam stopped to think carefully, and then continued. "They were going to fire some of us; we all knew that. Just as we knew that their arbitrary preference, not our competence, would decide who would go. My manager demonstrated his incompetence from the moment he was hired. He micromanaged everything into the ground—with disastrous results. He'd arrive late to my meetings, and then, unasked, he'd get up and start making speeches. Perhaps he thought he was bringing perspective, but for my team and me, it looked like grandstanding. It was damn embarrassing! The clients would shuffle around in their chairs, but he never got the message. I had to stand around until he finally finished."

"You felt anxious?"

"I was powerless. And I couldn't go over his head. Once I tried to tell him that two people presenting the same material interrupted the flow, but he took my comments personally. He accused me of being egotistical and threatened. Although he didn't want to learn anything, he wanted to control everything."

"What wonderful irony! People intent on controlling others give the game away. They have no control, and they know it. They live in terror of loss of control. When they are in authority, and they often are, they live in fear that others will find out, so they force their inse-curity on others by micromanaging."

"You also know about micromanagement!"

Aaron laughed out loud. "Who's the best micromanager or control freak you know, Sam?"

Sam was uncertain. "The devil?"

"The devil you say? Well, let me see if that concept fits into our discussion."

Aaron had a sparkle in his eye. "Probably, if you take into consideration that the devil is hatred, dishonesty, insincerity, meanness, aggression, deceit, and all the unconscious behavior you can think of that call for a false display of power, then it is possibly right. All of these are examples of behavior that is negative and out of control. And who manages these actions for you like a ruthless taskmaster?"

"I don't know. You said it is not the devil."

"Sam we're not talking about the devil tonight! You know as much of that concept as you know about God." Aaron looked Sam directly in the eye—there was no humor there. "Another time, we might address Him and him. Not tonight though, not directly, that is. All references to God are to illustrate a point only. You will find your Truth in your own time, when you have set your mind straight and when you start making conscious decisions, but not before then. How did you put it earlier tonight? Philosophical drivel is not what we want to engage in!

"No. It is not the devil who manages these actions. The answer is your mind. Your mindless, uncontrolled mind that has a mechanical mind of its own! One who micromanages others is a slave to his own mechanical mind, programmed by fear and distrust."

Both were quiet, listening to the sounds of the night.

Then Sam blurted, "Where is the way? How can we acquire this knowledge, for it seems to me that the whole human race suffers so much? Driven by fear and anxiety, why, we are all out of control!"

"You have taught yourselves to fake being in control, to pretend to be happy. But you live from your conditioned self—not your real self. Your conditioned self is a machine; a sophisticated machine that responds to impulses and stimuli with deadly accuracy. That is why the mass media is so powerful and why commercials lead you by the nose. The decision-making part of you is run by a mechanical mind!"

"Could we reprogram our minds with positive affirmations or something similar?"

"What good are the affirmations of a sleepwalker? Only when you choose to wake will affirmations sow seeds on fertile ground, then you will understand what control really is. Learning new patterns is hard work, because your mind wants to return to the sleep of the oblivious. You're in for the fight of your life!"

"Earlier you said this is our responsibility. It would have been wonderful if our parents taught us these principles, but they did not, because they did not know themselves?"

"Yes."

"How sad, how sad, when most of us operate out of control, and think it is hidden."

Sam's eyes went over the harbor, now in full view. *Where had the clouds gone?* He hadn't even noticed how clear it had become.

"Sam, before tonight, when you came to the mountain, what were some of the symptoms you regularly experienced?"

"Aaron, I don't know why you ask me questions, when you already know the answers."

"It is good for you to verbalize your thoughts. It makes them real, and you will remember them better. Tell me how you felt." Aaron insisted.

Sam remained quiet for a while as his thoughts went back to his most recent struggles. "I couldn't sleep anymore. I can't remember when I last slept. If I did doze, it was fitfully, and I awoke more exhausted than before going to sleep. And the headaches, the new, localized pain that drove me crazy! The pain preoccupied me. I was impatient and lost my temper easily. Karla got the worst of it. I can't even remember how long this went on, but it seemed to consume my life the last year. Nothing seemed worth the effort."

"Now, you remember that how you see the world, is therefore how it is, at least for you, and that you made it that way? That's why you called me to the mountain, your view of your life was self-defeating and very dark; you needed a change in perception, your model needed to be repaired."

"But circumstances . . ."

"Do not make you. They simply reveal who you really are. People lose control because they are not educated in these matters. They observe their role models, their parents, pastors, and teachers, and learn by example how to behave. Few of the role-models question their own powerlessness, so how can the pupils acquire insight into the process? Few suspect that there might be alternative interpretations, behaviors, and choices. Most accept the futile struggle as normal—a part of the human condition. It is called normal, but it is completely wrong."

"I see people living like this every day, Aaron!"

"Call it living, if you like. They don't really live, Sam. They stumble from day to day, praying that tomorrow will be better. But it never is. They don't recognize their responsibility. Few search for answers because they are asleep. They want their lives to improve, but they want to keep doing the same things; thinking the same things. It is ludicrous to repeat the same actions, but expect different results."

"You're reinforcing the dominance of thought processes again." Sam concentrated. "But if the law mandates that you are in control to the degree that you feel positive, and you're out of control to the degree that you feel negative . . ." he stopped, exasperated. "Well, it's a circular argument. We agree that most of the time people are negative and out of control, which makes positive thinking an almost impossible feat. We'd have to have superpowers!"

"No. Just conscious and aware. Instead, people don't ask themselves if their lives could be different! And if they do, they seek the advice of others equally uninformed. By fixing their attention on the problem, the problem, by law, remains a problem."

"How, I mean . . . Aaron?" Sam sounded incredulous.

"We'll take a walk in a few minutes to where we met tonight, and then I will elaborate on that point for you. But for now, let's talk about control." Aaron smiled. "Or the lack of it. Back to affirmations and programming, then."

"The affirmation solution never worked for me," Sam mused. "It always sounded so false; I had to convince me, and that was harder than anything else! It was one thing to say out loud that wonderful things were going to happen, but my gut usually told another story. And I avoided the positive enthusiasts, who also struck me as phonies. I could always identify the person who'd just returned from some seminar designed to transform them overnight."

"You say your gut told another story. Tell me what that means."

"It means that whenever I get that hollow feeling in the pit of my stomach, I pretty much know things will go wrong."

"How accurate is this gut feeling? Are you ever wrong?"

Sam pondered for a moment. "I don't think so, although I can't say I kept score."

"Nobody can lie to themselves or to each other, not truly. You see, Sam," Aaron stood right in front of him, "you cannot lie to the universe either. It is as you say, your mouth might pledge one thing, but if your feeling says another; there is incongruence between what you say and what you actually feel. Remember those futile feelings, where nothing is worth the effort or ever goes your way?"

Sam nodded absently.

"You might be frustrated, but to the universe none of this is a mystery. The universe is indifferent to what comes out of your mouth. It doesn't care if you can recite volumes of positive affirmations. It reads those frequencies, the vibrations of despair and anguish you try to hide behind positive affirmations. But they, these frequencies, give away how you really feel. The universe has no language, its language is energy, and that is universal.

"It reads energy; it interprets your mental fingerprint or energy ID. It follows the cues you give it. On the most fundamental level, everything—physical objects and intangible thoughts—is an expression of energy. Everything is energy in a continuous state of flux—alive and moving, and interacting. Similar objects and thoughts that resonate on the same frequency are attracted to one another. You can't see this with your naked eye, but it is a natural truism.

"On the one hand, therefore, you need to be able to look past your physical body to gain insight into this fantastic process called life. And yet, although it seems ethereal and mystical on another level, the entire process depends on the functioning of a law, or a rule, to manage it. In other words, it has a mechanical aspect to it. It is a beautiful union of the mechanical and the mystical, which is a characteristic of your world!

"There is the malleability, the potential, the absolute wonder of what you may create, but it is masterfully coupled with the independent will and desire of the human being. Hence the term 'mastering your destiny.' You become master of your destiny when you learn the Rules of the Game!"

Sam wanted to speak, but waited. One moment he thought he glimpsed total comprehension of Aaron's words. The next moment he felt he understood nothing.

"When you learn that the universe responds to what you generate by thought, you are on your way. The universe waits upon your data to unfold. It does not create out of nothingness. That is not its purpose. Its purpose is to read your energy frequency and, on the basis of like attracting alike, bring to you what you generate, in the form of similar thoughts, events, people, and circumstances. The energy origin is the thought, the thought that has the potential to create your heart's desire or wreak havoc! The thought begins in your head."

Sam nodded.

"And all thoughts generate emotion, don't they? Even if the thought is inconsequential, it still produces some kind of emotion?"

Sam nodded again, unsure.

"The literal pathway is thought," Aaron pointed to his head, "which travels to the heart chakra, or energy center where the thought is converted into an emotion." He put his hand over his heart and looked at Sam, "Emotion is centered in the heart. Is it true that all emotions generate some kind of feeling?" This time he waited for Sam to respond.

"I don't know. Is it?"

"Work with me, Sam. You are the one who needs to understand this. When you experience joy in your heart, how does that make you feel?"

Sam considered his reply. "Happy, I guess."

"That happy feeling comes from your solar plexus. The energy of joy in your heart is sent along to the solar plexus where the joy is converted into a feeling of happiness." This time Aaron moved his hand down to a spot below his heart and above the navel. "The feeling literally leaves your body from the solar plexus, converted into a frequency—the language of the universe! Frequency is what the universe reads, Sam! It interprets the frequency that you sent out, which originated from the thought you had. This is the mechanical aspect of the universe. It waits for your signal, your frequency. And on the basis of what you literally asked for, it begins to attract and produce in kind."

"That is how we create our own realities?" Sam was suddenly enormously excited by the implications of what he just heard. "I see it now; we do it with how we think!"

Aaron smiled broadly. "You are no different from a radio station that continuously sends out signals. The universe responds to all of the signals you generate. Some are weak, and others very strong, but it never makes a mistake!" Aaron had a mischievous look on his face. "There is one problem, though."

Sam waited.

"You can tune in to any radio station, or television station for that matter, because they never change their frequencies. You depend on that fact; that's how you know what frequency to set the dial on." Aaron again moved his gaze to the dark ocean with the lighted ships on it.

His voice dropped very low, and Sam had to lean forward to hear him. "With all the different emotions and feelings you experience in just one hour, can you imagine the spectrum of thoughts these must come from? You might fluctuate from states of euphoria to deep sadness. In this hapless journey you pass through the barren regions of 'whatever,' 'who cares?' or 'stuff happens' so often, it has been inculcated into your popular idiom because almost everybody owns a piece of real estate in this miserable no-man's-land. And some have pitched their tents to live here permanently, because they have not learned that no one cares if you don't! It is one of the saddest self-fulfilling prophecies of humankind."

"Aaron? What is the rule that supports what you just told me? Is this the Law of Cause and Effect?"

Aaron took a deep breath through his nose, and then let the air slowly escape through his mouth. "You came to the mountain tonight because you felt you could not live one more day, not one more moment of what you thought life had in store for you."

"Yes." Sam didn't look at him.

"It was not what life had in store for you that you couldn't handle. Life was simply demonstrating to you how big the inner disaster was you had created for yourself. Your reaction was to choose the cliff. You thought that you could erase the past with one leap into the night. Your deeper desire, however, was to understand how you arrived at this desperate station in your life. So you called me. I am here not to point out your mistakes, but to illustrate the depth of your desire to manage and finally master your life. I am here to help you know that you are responsible for every thought, every action. And I am here to show you how to do it right.

"Every thought is the cause of a circumstance in your life, even if you cannot see it. The Law of Cause and Effect is a fundamental rule of the game. I think you are ready to play."

▲ ▲ ▲

Two Thousand Years and Counting

*A*aron and Sam leaned on the low wall overlooking the harbor and the ocean. The harbor was in full view and the ocean danced with glistening phosphor. The moon daubed gold and silver splashes of light over the restless surface, as if a child artist had passed by and carelessly dropped paint splotches from her bucket on her way to . . . Where? Perhaps she slipped across to the other side of the world, to another ocean, or a still lake, or to a quiet desert, to cover it in midnight white.

Sam smiled at his own thoughts. The moon was a playful little girl to him. He was sure she had a mop of unruly, coppery-yellow curls. She had skipped across the bay tonight in a hurry, not noticing how much of her gold and silver paint she had dripped on the harbor. She was already off to find her next playground in the night sky of the universe.

"You are quite the poet, Sam," Aaron whispered, his gaze on the ocean.

"When I was a child, I never felt good enough." Sam closed his eyes, remembering. "I didn't relate to my parents, and my only sister is many years my senior. She was always a stranger. She came to my daughter's funeral. I hadn't seen her before that day for over ten years, and I was surprised she showed up at all. I didn't realize she cared enough."

Aaron straightened and looked at Sam. "You called her your daughter for the first time tonight."

For a brief moment he considered Aaron's words, and then his resistance crumbled. Sam began to cry. He sobbed with grief, and gave himself over to it. For the first time, he let the pain pour out and allowed it to run its course for what felt like a very long time. Aaron watched him silently, neither interfering nor helping.

After several minutes, Sam's tears began to subside. He became conscious of Aaron leaning over the wall looking into the darkness, and of a scuttling sound on the rock-faced cliff beneath them. "Those are dassies," said Aaron, pointing. "They look like big rodents, but strangely, their closest relative is the elephant."

Involuntarily, Sam smiled at the zoology lesson. He was thinking about the unfamiliar lightness in his chest, as if there were too much space; he thought his heart might be floating in his chest cavity.

Finally he spoke, "The baby's death drove Karla out of her mind. She accused me of the most terrible things, and she said only a monster . . . I didn't understand why I couldn't think of her as my daughter."

"It was easier that way, Sam. When we identify with anything, it becomes personal. Calling your daughter 'the baby' established the distance you needed to disassociate. As a temporary coping measure, it worked. It was a form of self-preservation that perhaps your wife could not understand. She had the same trauma and pain as you, but she experienced it very differently. She had an attachment to her pain. She had carried the baby for just over eight months; the bond created by the umbilical cord is greatly underestimated. There is a continuous exchange of information, thoughts, feelings, and emotions between the mother and the child she carries. The baby appears helpless as it emerges into the world, but it knows, Sam. It knows."

"Aaron, I couldn't say Karla's name either. Why?"

"You were planning your end tonight, Sam. You needed to disassociate from everyone who meant anything to you. You tried to cut the emotional ties so you could find enough courage to leap off the cliff." Aaron spoke matter-of-factly. "I repeat, not everybody who feels overwhelmed by life ends up on the edge of a cliff. Many people lack so much interest in their lives that they accept what they see as their fate. When they go to their graves, however, their departure is harsh because they never found that innate inner peace; they didn't know where to look."

"You don't mean in a church, do you?"

"Sam, your assumption that inner peace is found in a church is a conditioned response. Our meeting tonight is not to judge what others do or which path they find themselves on. But here is a truth that will help you to distinguish between what is right or wrong for you: spiritual growth is an intensely personal affair; it cannot be collective. All attempts in the past to make it collective have resulted in dogmatic teachings by humans with their own agendas. It has become one of the biggest battlefields of strife and hatred in the history of mankind. Terrible egos rule the world." Aaron was silent for a while. Then he asked, "Amid all of humans' hatred and strife, what do you think limits God, Sam?"

Sam didn't reply.

"Only his name." Aaron said quietly. "People murder to protect their own vanity, their own sense of importance. Their arrogance and ignorance are equal. And those who believe their salvation to be dependent on holy wars, or who subtly exert social pressures on the unbelievers—they are gone from the game long ago. Their smugness serves them naught in the end. They don't even know that they're not playing anymore.

"These groups proclaim the message of love, but they act out of hatred and intolerance. In defending their beliefs, they have to be right no matter what the cost. They don't love their neighbor, because they first choose who is worthy of being their neighbor. They sit in judgment of others, and never look at themselves. The Rules of the Game don't allow for this, Sam. They're all benched."

"Why are we talking about religion? I understood that we were specifically not discussing it."

Aaron kept his eyes on the bay, sprinkled with lighted ships, as he answered, "You ask a significant question. Our meeting tonight is intended to bring perspective and insight into what you call religion, but is really your quest for your spiritual self, to know who you are. If your essence is not spirit, Sam, then what could it be? We agreed that conscious awareness is the key that unlocks the truth for every human being. How then, would it be possible for us not to address what has imprisoned you so?"

"Are you saying there is no place for organized religion in this world?"

"People are where they are in the journey of life, Sam. Some are born understanding that God is not in a building. Others choose the collective experience because their spirit craves the support of like-minded people. That choice is neither right nor wrong. It simply is; every individual is always where he or she needs to be.

"But you chose to move on from the collective a long time ago. Our conversation concerning religion and spirituality is to further your insight, not to judge others. This question has always figured large in your life, since you couldn't be made to fit, ever. You were the little tree that broke the confines of the pot they tried to plant you in even before you were born, hence your feelings of discomfort from the time you could think. Now, however, you are in the forest and you have to grow, on your own, as everyone who wants to grow must. For others, the cosmos may appear to be in chaos. But those who can look beneath the surface see the law operate undisturbed by human lunacy.

"We can use organized religion as an example of the rule you and I talked about earlier, the great Law of Cause and Effect. It is the mechanical aspect of all the laws that are underestimated by all. There is no benefit in pretending anything. Every action has its equal and opposite reaction. And it functions independently of the preference of man, but without a doubt according to his thoughts and actions, that is the mechanical component.

"Conscious beings find pleasure in this law, because the outcome is their preference. Unconscious beings derive no pleasure from feeling at the mercy of luck, or of the gods' arbitrary favor. Indeed, it must be very difficult to plot a course in life according to so much happenstance."

Sam nodded, "Yes, it was."

Aaron continued, "Let us closely examine the operation of Cause and Effect in religion—our example. Supposing someone covets his neighbor's wife, but enters his pew faithfully every Sunday. His presence in church does not revoke the desire or the deed. Every secret desire results in either fulfilling of the need or denial of the same. It clearly has implicit and explicit consequences.

"Desires fulfilled under cover of darkness grow to a terrible drive that consumes the mind and blinds the senses, thus rendering moderate people reckless and out of control. Unfulfilled dark desires lead to frustration and irritability; a general discontent with life, with a particularly unpleasant outcome. It disallows the perpetrator the first step toward illumination and growth, for he will find it impossible to love himself. Pretending to love yourself under these circumstances, whether in a church, a mosque, or a temple, is a total sham.

"It is now two thousand years and counting, Sam. When the Jesus entity was here, he taught the same principles; he taught that you always reap what you sow. Do you think that law has anything to do with how we behave? With how we treat others?

"Do you think we can get away with what we hide inside? Who sees into your heart? Who knows your deepest thoughts and hidden desires? You do! Meanwhile, most of us hope to God that no one else does."

"No one can lie to the universe, you said," Sam offered, amazed at the clarity with which Aaron spoke.

"But we spend such time and energy pretending!" said Aaron. "No, it is impossible to lie, even to ourselves. The Law of Correspondence demands congruence between your inner and outer reality. And the Law of Cause and Effect means that you alone are responsible for your thoughts, words, and deeds. These are two fundamental Rules of the Game. You cannot set the conditions. You cannot design your own version of the law. Nor can you claim that God will forgive you for your sins, while you consciously repeat them. Such behavior ignores the rule.

"Humans choose to manipulate their interpretation of grace. They choose to believe that their bad behavior does not matter, for grace allows them to be forgiven. If people did not choose this interpretation, they would work to know and better themselves. Instead, this interpretation of grace lets them behave as they please. Again, devotion to anything is meaningless if your behavior does not change. No behavior can change unless a change occurs in the thought process.

"Do you now see how transparent it is when one declares himself a devotee but has a foul temper or constantly belittles others around him, including his offspring? It is completely inconsistent with the Rules of the Game."

"What is grace then?" Sam asked in wonder.

"Grace is a state. Grace is arriving at an oasis in the wilderness and knowing you have found the source of Life. Only an honest heart and an open mind can reach this place. For it is an inward journey, not an outward one.

"In Grace you know that sitting beside the well with good intentions won't quench your thirst. Grace is leaning over the water to scoop Life up, and seeing your own reflection as it is, perhaps for the first time. Grace is to take 'Know Thyself' into your heart, not into your mouth, where it can be spat out again. Grace is insight into the magnificent process of universal interconnectedness.

"In the state of Grace, you recognize that you are part of the whole, but a worthy part. If you believe yourself unworthy, your behavior must demonstrate that belief. Small wonder humans don't take responsibility for their actions, and this is the real reason why so few invest time in self-improvement; they don't see it as their liability. It is God's, for they have been taught that they are unworthy. Their unworthiness is the escape clause for their often reckless deeds and untamed thoughts. Why would they take responsibility, if God knows their weakness and will forgive them for it?

"When you are in Grace, you no longer sluggishly attribute your negativity to human nature. You become response able and discover that happiness is a choice. And then you choose it! You do not expect others to make you happy; you recognize this as your personal mission. And you understand above all, that every little step you take forward, benefits the entire race. That is Grace. It is a genuine personal effort that allows a human being to glimpse and experience the divine. Seeing this humbles you and gives you hope. Not bogus strength, but strength that leads to authentic individuality—no longer dependent on the approval of others. Grace is above all to recognize God in everything and in all people."

"Then a person arrives," Sam mused aloud.

"This is not an arrival of any kind, Sam; it is not a 'saddling off'; rather it is 'saddling up.' It finally opens the door to start your journey toward the Absolute." Aaron's voice was soft and reverent.

Sam stayed silent, hoping that the night would never end, that Aaron would never stop speaking. Aaron was his Sherpa, leading him through the valley of darkness and away from that terrible cliff. He didn't want this experience to end.

Finally he spoke, "I hope to remember of all of this."

"Don't try. Memorizing information on this level leads only to confusion. You are not looking for more facts, but once you understand a concept, you own it. You don't have to commit it to memory. In this case, it will come through personal experience."

"I will have a hard time telling others about you, Aaron." He thought it sounded a bit lame, but didn't know what else to say.

Aaron shrugged and dismissed the reference to him, "Tonight is about you. It is about your life, your struggles, and the people closest to you. You have more than enough to take you further." He continued, "The unworthiness you felt as a child never went away."

Sam laughed gently, "No, not until tonight." He was delighted with the ease he felt talking to Aaron about his deepest feelings. "I thought I had learned how to manage it. But, because my parents used guilt on me, it was very easy for others to recognize how easily I could be manipulated. Every time they succeeded, I seemed to shrink a little more. Even at six feet two, I was often small."

"See how understanding benefits us?" They sat down again, simultaneously, legs stretched out in front of them, their arms folded across their chests. "This law determines the outcome of everything with predictable accuracy, Sam." Aaron closed his eyes, in deep thought. "You cannot instill fear in children and expect them to be brave. You cannot convince them of their worthlessness and then wonder why they are timid, afraid, and don't trust themselves, or others. Feelings of worthlessness often show up in adults as constant abuse of power. It stems from the same fear of insignificance that cannot result in respect, but leads to distrust and more fear.

"You cannot protect a child by taking his responsibility, his learning, away from him, and then expect him to grow into a responsible adult. Action always equals reaction. There is no other way; you must start with the basics. Even if you cannot trace the problem back to the origin, or if it is not obvious, it does not mean there is no connection.

"But the 'rational' laugh at this idea. They do not know the depth of their own ignorance, because proof must precede belief. Anything they do not own, they ignore or reject. If they have a religious leaning, they tenuously fluctuate between allegorical interpretation of their holy books and stubborn worship of science in the changing world of fact. They never find the seldom-traveled inner path that leads to the cool, babbling brook.

"Such people are almost always tired and worn out. They rarely discover their intuitive self; it doesn't stand a chance against the hard outer shell screaming for validation. They prefer to associate with the deafening masses engaged in their next study, to be disproved in short order by another intellectual who craves admiration and the spotlight. They serve their egos harder than they serve their gods."

"Do you mean God?"

"No, Sam. If you have not yet discovered the inner path of authentic—not contrived humility—you are worshipping the golden calf. These are the gods. Those mining the gold of self-righteousness pay homage to the gods even as they look toward heaven, only they don't know it. That is the tragedy. Their arrogance rules their lives. It is very hard to learn something new when the consciousness, like stale bread, becomes crusty and hard.

"Your world has been created such that the more you learn about it, the better you understand yourself, and vice versa. The one depends on the other, for interdependence has been designed to lead you to self-illumination. But you have to care enough! No one cares if you don't—another certainty of this rule. If you care enough to investigate your world, the universe lets you into its secrets to the exact degree that you exert the effort. Action, reaction. Action, reaction." His voice was a soft murmur.

The silence between them was relaxed and easy. Sam had also closed his eyes in comfortable reflection, where nothing was expected of him. He could see it all so clearly now. He saw how his feelings of unworthiness had held him back all these years, not because of what others had denied him, but because of what he had denied himself. He saw himself repeating the self-defeating behavior he had inherited from his parents. He saw and understood that although he had the capacity to feel very deeply, he was a closed book to others.

He had made it impossible for others to get to know him. He had cut himself off from the world to protect himself, and years of conditioning had reinforced this habit. It had become a necessary coping skill, expressed internally as self-pity and externally in periods of loaded, stony silence, during which he had expected others to come to their senses. They never did.

Karla saw through the facade very early on and yet loved the real person. But when she needed him, he was unable to overcome his debilitating belief that he was a victim, and so he watched her disintegrate in front of his eyes. He was helpless to assist her; he didn't even know how to deal with himself, for he believed he was getting what he deserved. He had no idea how tightly invested he was in his sense of unworthiness. Unworthiness is the miserable guide that leads all its victims to defeatist behavior.

He thought of his career and how hard he had tried in the past to measure up to the expectations of others. That was the problem: they were never his expectations. Out of his feelings of lack, he had devoted years trying to please others, and had never learned how to please him. He had chased the elusive dreams of others, driven by an external urgency that had frustrated him and drained him of his motivation.

Action and reaction: a fundamental rule of the game. Sam considered its application. You cannot plant deceit and reap truth. You cannot feel unworthy and experience recognition. You cannot plot the demise of another and thrive yourself. You cannot wage war in the name of peace. You cannot gain respect where there is self-hatred.

He let the images run across his mind—they were crystal clear. Why did he not know this before or understand its application? That was the problem. The information was not unknown, but until tonight it was theory only; it rarely reached to the level of daily living so he could get back in the game. Life has a beautiful, flowing rhythm to it, undisturbed by the schemes and plans of mere mortals. Life keeps moving gently, coursing its way along the path of universal justice.

This Law of Cause and Effect demonstrates all the thoughts and desires of the human race without preference or judgment by producing circumstances to match. Those who awaken and learn from the outcome of unwanted results endeavor not to make the same mistakes again. Others fall into depression and frustration, beseeching the God who had forsaken them, or pray for a reprieve, confessing their unworthiness, still believing it is God's thing; thus they seldom stop to ask if they have some responsibility to assume."

Again, the comfortable silence enveloped them for a long time, and then Aaron asked. "Do you know what prayer is, Sam?"

Sam awoke from his reverie. He knew himself to be young again, and he felt a great excitement stirring within.

Aaron spoke, "Prayer is an inner commitment to find and implement a better way. It is a focused approach toward correct action."

"And it really helps," finished Sam.

"Absolutely. It is, interestingly enough, the only way to help your-self! Prayers are answered according to the devotion you put into them, not from a position of unworthiness, but exactly the opposite." Aaron's voice resonated with urgency. "Sam, look at the impossibility of what you asked for in the past, and so many ask for today. They say they are unworthy, but they ask for an outcome that does not match their inner state. They are asking God to break a rule in this game so they can have it their way. It is acceptance of responsibility; it is acceptance of the load, and most of all it is a forward momentum driven by that internal divine spark. That is prayer."

"Cause and Effect again," Sam said quietly.

"Always. See now how Cause and Effect goes hand in hand with the Law of Correspondence? It drives the human race crazy," he said calmly, "because they want change, but expect it to come from out there someplace!"

"The chameleon thing?"

Aaron laughed. "The opposite is true for you. Your thoughts cause your reality. Your thoughts call to you all the people and circumstances that vibrate in harmony with who you essentially are. Thoughts are the causes; circumstances are, therefore, the outcomes. Action and reaction. The quality of the thoughts, the vibrational level, determines your energy ID or fingerprint. That is the inner level that manifests outwardly. Are you following me, Sam?"

Sam nodded, mesmerized and in tune.

"There is only one little catch. You have to be a genius to do this." He nodded his head slowly when he saw the expression on Sam's face. "Yes. To know how to create your own reality effectively, it helps if you are a genius."

"Shit!"

Aaron let that go, "Why do you let that disturb you unnecessarily?" His eyes left Sam's face for a moment and swept over the bay, slowly disappearing behind the clouds again. "The good news is that there is only one difference between genius and mediocrity."

Sam waited, a slow smile creeping around his mouth. "What is it, Aaron?"

"Focus," he said slowly. "Focus makes the difference. The difference between mediocrity and genius is focus, and the mystery of how to create is securely locked up in focus."

▲　　▲　　▲

Mediocre Geniuses

*A*aron looked up at the ceiling of clouds above them. "This mountain is an unusual place, sitting here right at the foot of this impressive continent where the cold Atlantic and the warm Indian oceans meet." He looked at Sam, eyeing him curiously. "Have you ever thought about that?"

Sam laughed, trying to hide his impatience. "About what, Aaron? Africa or the mountain?"

"Both." Aaron too was amused. "Sam, have you not noticed how important it is to break the flow of information from time to time? You need time to assimilate what we talked about earlier, but I know you are impatient."

"So, first we had a lesson in zoology, and now geography gets a turn."

"Let's go back to the main area where the restaurant is. It is getting very damp."

"We're on the move again," Sam said under his breath as he turned to follow Aaron who was already striding away. How remarkable that Aaron never asked for permission. Once he made up his mind, his style was to state his intention, then he followed through on his words.

"The mountain is not only unusual because it looks like a table with its flat surface," Aaron said over his shoulder, "but also because it is home to extraordinary flora found nowhere else in the world."

Sam listened, calmly. He knew the conversation was going some-where.

"An unusual setting, in an unusual night." Aaron kept talking as he walked. He didn't look back to see if Sam were following. "Here we are on top of a mountain at the tip of Africa. Think about that! To the south of us there is only endless ocean, and to the north an incredible mass of land—a land from which the people could learn some very valuable lessons. Some did and others still haven't, as always."

"What do you mean?"

"This is one of the richest continents on the planet, and yet signifi-cant and repeated famines kill many thousands yearly. Why?" Aaron did-n't wait for an answer. "The great Law of Cause and Effect admonishes that people cannot pillage the land and expect it to yield a handsome crop. If you take from the land—in farming or mineral riches—you must return in equal measure what you have taken, either in labor or in goodwill to the people. Disrespect of this law punishes the people of the land severely and creates massive imbalances that cannot be healed overnight. It accentuates the disparities that exist between those who prosper and those who suffer, but it also reveals the purpose of polarities in this world as instruction and ultimate illumination of the soul."

"You learn about your soul from the land?"

"Everything is there for your instruction. Those who live off the land and have not yet advanced," he gave a little laugh, "or not yet succumbed to levels where the intellect demands a definition of God, contentedly find their gods in nature. They cower from thunder and lightning, fearing the displeasure of their gods. But in the morning they worship the sun, grateful for his forgiveness. They learn from their own experiences cast against a backdrop they understand; there is a special beauty in such devotion for it lacks treachery.

"But if others force upon them their version of civilization, which here in Africa is almost always accompanied by a hefty dose of salvation, they cannot fathom the meaning. They nod and smile, but their hearts are not reached, far less their souls. This is one harvest human hands—however good the intention—cannot gather. What arrogance convinces civilized man that he should intervene in the growth and development of others? How can you know light if you haven't experienced darkness? Your feet might have to blister on the hot coals of hell before you see the gates of heaven. It is the experience of these polarities which facilitates growth.

"When sorrow ends, happiness and joy need no explanation; the heart readily embraces the light because it knows the opposite through experience. Knowledge without experience has little value; it is experience alone that allows you to own knowledge, nothing else. And experience cannot be sold. You can't even give it away, because it isn't yours to give. Polarities allow you to know there is an alternative, and to see the contrast, and contrast is what affords you the opportunity to choose."

Sam had caught up to Aaron, who had slowed his pace. He felt the cold and shivered uncontrollably. He stuck his hands in his pockets, pulled his shoulders up against the chill and blew hard through his mouth. He watched his breath vaporize and carefully contemplated Aaron's words. He wanted to remember every word, yet, strangely, none of the words sounded alien to him. Indeed, the moment Aaron expressed a thought, Sam felt as though he could have said it, and then he wondered why he hadn't. It was as though the information had been sleeping in his consciousness forever. The night was getting stranger and stranger.

"So you're beginning to like the philosophical drivel?" Aaron chuckled.

"It makes so much sense," Sam said, shivering. "I guess when we were at the cliff tonight, I protested against being rescued, but I said nothing about being preached to, so you seized that gap!"

Aaron began walking more quickly, easily finding his way in the dark. "Let's see. It is past midnight and we're atop a magnificent mountain, right at the tip of a continent where two oceans converge. Very unusual, yes?"

In the darkness behind, Sam nodded.

"This mountain is the habitat of exquisite fine bush, silver trees, and some beautiful orchids. It is too dark to see them right now, but some are so rare that they aren't found anywhere else in the world. This is also the home to the ghost bullfrog, another little fellow that lives only on this mountain. This place is so special that they are thinking of declaring it a World Heritage Site."

Sam stopped, grabbing Aaron's arm from behind. "How do you know all this?" he demanded. "Aaron, will you tell me who you are before the night is over?" Sam moved into Aaron's path and held his hands together as if in prayer.

Aaron smiled gently. "You know who I am."

"No, I don't!" He looked urgently at Aaron "Do I?"

"Why, Sam, you stopped shivering. You're not cold anymore!"

Sam looked at his arms and then at his body. He felt fine. It was cold outside, but somehow he didn't feel it anymore.

"Did you . . .?" Sam didn't understand, just a few moments ago he had been shaking with the cold!

"Sam, you just made your own miracle."

"How did I do that?" He wasn't cold at all anymore!

"Well, what happened here occurred unconsciously on your part, but I happened to witness it."

"What?" Sam could not stand the suspense any longer. "What happened?"

"A genius just quit being mediocre, fulfilled his destiny briefly and became a genius again." Aaron looked at Sam's face and, for the first time, let out a deep belly laugh that shook his entire body. "Sam . . ." Aaron couldn't speak through his fits of laughter.

"This is funny?" Sam was indignant. "I fail to see the humor in . . ." His face changed, and then lit up as understanding dawned. "Oh my God, how clever you are! I walked right into it and I can see it now! It is focus! You led my attention away from the cold by talking about the mountain and its creatures. When I began to focus on the uniqueness of our meeting and our surroundings, my attention was diverted and the cold disappeared." Suddenly, Sam was unsure. "Oh God, could it really be that simple?"

"Yes, Sam. Creation is precisely that simple because it follows the Law of Energy. That's why our discussion started with energy tonight. And that is also why I have repeated some important concepts to you. The human being learns through the process of spaced repetition. I know if I repeat important information to you with certain intervals, you will remember." Aaron looked delightedly at Sam, "You always get what you concentrate on, Sam!

"Mind and body is one thing, joined at the hip, if you like." He laughed. "Wherever the mind goes, the body has to follow. It has no choice; it must do the bidding of the mind."

Sam felt incredible, intense emotion rushing through his body. For a fleeting moment he thought that he couldn't bear what he felt and understood in that moment, but he kept his eyes fixed on Aaron. He thought of Karla and their child and then felt the heavy weight of regret drop on him again. He looked at Aaron for help.

Aaron shook his head slowly. "It cannot be undone, Sam. The pain you feel is significant of the change happening. You are shedding a part of you that cannot be restored, because it is evolving. Change is painful because it is letting go of the old and the known, but it is what facilitates the opening to new possibilities—just like death and birth. You understand?"

Sam's nod was almost imperceptible.

"Your little girl played her part in this life." There was deep compassion in his voice. "Her death led you here, led you to independence, and freed your mind. She has done that very well. There is nothing to regret."

Sam's eyes filled with tears. "Karla . . ."

Aaron lightly touched Sam's shoulder. "That is not over yet. Come, we're almost there," he continued. "See the faint light in the distance?" He pointed through the fog to a shimmering ahead of them. "The chairs will be a lot more comfortable."

The fog swirled imperceptibly as they approached the clearing outside the restaurant. They each took a chair and sat down. Sam struggled with a myriad of emotions. Scenes from his past played in his mind's eye. He understood why he had assumed the role of victim so frequently. But he was also excited with his newly found knowledge and insights. Aaron remained his tranquil self, but Sam knew he was waiting.

The night was very dark. They were cocooned in layers of the mist and fog. Sam did not know how tomorrow or the rest of his life would play out, but he felt a confidence he had never known before. Something significant had changed and he tried to identify the source of the change.

What was it? The way he looked at his life, his paradigm? Was it the death of their daughter or his marriage to Karla? Had the meaning of these changed? Could all of this have changed in a few short hours? Was it possible to come from a place of self-loathing and self-destruction to this place of peace, even grace, in this short time?

Before tonight, everything had been about me, but now I feel such a deep compassion for everything, and all people. How had this transformation happened?

"When you change your paradigm, everything changes. It is no mystery," Aaron spoke. "That is why it is so important to be conscious of what you are thinking. You only become aware of your thoughts—the conscious ones as well as that unrelenting undercurrent that runs through your mind—when you become aware. You become awake and aware to yourself first, then to the world."

"That is why we struggle so much?"

"Yes, Sam. The human race struggles because it does not understand the enigma of creation." Aaron, his voice soft and deep, was in deep reverie. "The enigma of creation is that you get what you focus on. Where you put your attention is where the creation happens, always. It really doesn't matter how intellectual you are or whether you believe this or not; the universe pays it no heed. It is incapable of caring about your personal preferences, for it follows only the immutable Law of Energy. The language of the universe is energy, Sam." They were both quiet, listening to the muffled sounds of the night.

"Hear that?" Far away and barely audible came a faint croaking. "That's the ghost bullfrog."

Sam sighed contentedly. He focused on absorbing the magnificence of what was happening. From moment to moment he concentrated on the wonder of the meeting. He would start to ask Aaron about that, to get more clarity, but every time he was about to ask the question it seemed irrelevant. Instead he said, "Aaron, the average person will not easily understand the concept of energy. Most people will see that as a tremendous load to carry, too big a responsibility."

"We are not talking about the average person tonight, Sam. We're talking about you. Is this too hard for you?"

Sam considered his answer carefully. It was pointless trying to deceive someone who knew the words before Sam could speak them. He thought about the concept of creating his own reality, and of the role his upbringing had played in how he experienced his world.

From his father he had learned that he wasn't good enough. Occasional attention couldn't compensate for the overwhelming inadequacies he felt around him. As an adult, he had recognized intellectually that his father had projected his own failures onto Sam, the child, but the damage had seemed irreversible. His feelings of inadequacy were established and cultivated through his parents' example. This became his model, his way of life supposedly hidden under the veneer of adulthood. Sam closed his eyes to revisit the scenarios that had shaped his character and personality.

From his mother he had learned silence and distance. Her primary defense was emotional defection into a deadly quietness. Her method of attack was a slow, terrible aggression expertly used as punishment. Silence was a weapon she wielded with skill and precision, and it never failed to find its target; it was impossible to argue with a wall. Attempts at meaningful conversation were abandoned with frustration. The wall had staring eyes, but no tongue; it couldn't or wouldn't speak. His defenses grew. He was armed against the onslaught of the world with everything negative, disguised as guarded optimism. The world was a dangerous place where nobody could be trusted and self-preservation was the name of the game.

Sam shook his head a little, his eyes still closed. Where does Karla fit into any of this? She is so unlike him. Or is she? He opened his eyes and looked at Aaron. "Is she like me?"

"What do you think, Sam? What have you learned tonight?"

"No." He frowned in concentration. "I'm not sure. She has a different personality! She is the one who always supports me when life gets me down. Even when we were children, she was the one who could laugh when I couldn't! Only since our daughter's death has she retreated into depression . . ." His voice trailed off as he grappled for insight.

"Keep on the subject, Sam. Do not be distracted by external characteristics. What you have in common, the reason for your attraction to each other is your level of consciousness."

"The Law of Attraction. You're saying that we were essentially in a similar place and therefore . . .?"

Aaron leaned forward. "I see you see that your consciousnesses complement each other, and you are equal in understanding and insight. This congruence gives a couple opportunities to learn from one another. The peaks and valleys may not be exactly equal, but that makes it interesting, and provides space for growth on both sides. If you had a partner very far ahead, or far behind you in her comprehension, the relationship could not last. The reasons are obvious. Despite the differences and unique approaches, the sameness is definite."

"Is learning from each other a given, then?"

"Nothing is ever a given. The learning exists as pure potential. How much is accepted from each other depends on the free will and choice of the individuals. In some relationships one party grows in leaps and bounds, while the other stays stagnant.

"A person who doesn't grow remains in one place not through lack of potential or opportunity, but through lack of interest. And, subconsciously, that is exercising choice. In this respect, not choosing is the same as declining the opportunity to grow."

"Aaron, how many people really accomplish this?" Sam felt despondent.

"Those who care enough will learn it once they understand the benefits, Sam. You said the average person would have difficulty working with this information."

Sam nodded.

"And you know why."

"Negative conditioning?"

"That, and unawareness. People are not aware that they are focused on the negative. How can you change anything that you are not aware of?"

Sam sat up suddenly, astonishment on his face. "That means that we have most things backwards."

"How so?" Aaron watched him with veiled amusement.

"It is inevitably so. Since we get what we concentrate on, then I understand what you meant when earlier tonight you said that I think about my problems all the time. You said that was my problem. Thus, if you sit on your problems and brood over them, then by law you'll be compounding them, because you're giving them your attention!"

Aaron's face was immobile. "But aren't you supposed to think about your problems? How can you solve your problems if you don't think about them? Surely that can't be avoided?"

"What?"

Aaron wore his poker face "You have to think about your problems. Who solves your problems, if not you? God, perhaps?"

"No!" Sam jumped up, unable to contain himself. "No! Change your focus! You have to put your attention on what you want, not on what you don't want!" He paced back and forth, in front of Aaron who sat motionless. "It has to be that way, for that way follows the Law of Energy, Attraction, and the whole troop! Come on, Aaron! That is how it is, right?"

"But what is the real significance, Sam? If you have to change your focus and take your attention away from the problem, where will you put it?"

Sam stared at him speechless for a moment. "On the solution, you rascal!" he laughed out loud. "You have to focus on the solution!"

Aaron smiled.

Sam continued somberly, "Is that what Einstein meant when he said we cannot solve a problem on the same level it was created on?" Tilting his head to one side, he considered his own question. Then, "Yes, that must be it. That is exactly what he meant! I know it!"

"Good thinking, Sam. You have to come to another level: the level of the solution." Aaron smiled broadly at the joy in Sam's face. "And why? Because solution thinking has a completely different energy level than problem thinking. Focusing on the problem, confirms exactly that, the problem. Focusing on the solution invites untold possibilities for healing of both the problem and your mind. That's why."

Silence. They both just sat. Sam felt an unfamiliar excitement. The possibilities were endless. He could not contain his excitement. He looked at Aaron who had his legs stretched out in front of him in familiar pose, arms crossed over his chest. He was looking off into the distance somewhere past Sam, but Sam knew he was aware of every move and every thought. What an extraordinary man!

"No problem has a life force of its own." Aaron looked back at Sam as he spoke. "Always remember this."

"With you I just never know! Just when I think I get it, you . . ."

Aaron cut him short. "It is an advanced concept, but it explains the futility of endless worry, the favorite, mindless pastime of the unaware. It also holds the secret to healing. And this will serve you well to know, Sam.

"In order to keep a problem alive, you have to give it your life force. Your life force is the same as your attention. Your attention is life support for problems. When you withdraw your attention, the problem dies.

"This principle is so difficult, so much harder to understand. And it is even harder to put into practice because people are attached to their problems. Indeed, many are defined by their problems, and to take that away is like stealing their identity. Remember then, everything is energy. Everything vibrates and moves, is alive and has a frequency, including thoughts." Aaron looked at Sam who appeared lost in thought.

"Sam?"

Sam rested his folded arms on his knees, his eyes on the ground in front of him. "I'm with you," he said imperceptibly.

"Everything has a life force, except a problem," Aaron continued. "For a problem is not concrete; it is a concept of something, a perception, which means it is thought-based."

"What about the problem of relationships? What about Karla and me?"

"Neither Karla nor you is the problem. The way you both think about each other and the resultant difficulties you experienced, that is the problem. If you change your problem approach to her and your relationship, the problem will begin to dissipate. It has no choice for it gets its energy supply, its existence as a problem from you. When you follow the solution approach, possibilities for healing will become visible. Right now, they are hidden because you keep them hidden. Come, we have unfinished business." They stood in unison, facing each other.

"Sam, the wonder of the universe is the inseparability of the person and his or her world. Until you discover this secret, you live in confusion, anger, and frustration. By your own decree, you live in a world of joy or misery. Your world is made manifest by your thoughts. When you become a conscious, aware human being, you discover from an inner source the deepest secret of all. You discover that vibration creates your world from thought, and that your world exists in testimony to your beliefs. And you discover that all the clues and all the signs you need to live consciously and in harmony are manifested in your immediate world around you. They face you openly, every day."

▲   ▲   ▲

Like a Child

"Where to now?" It still was very dark. Since he wasn't wearing his watch, Sam had no idea of the time.

"It is three thirty. We will return to the cliff where we met tonight," said Aaron already up and moving.

Sam smiled at Aaron's back, struck by how easily he had been following this man around on the mountain all night. This behavior was out of character for him, but tonight at least he was content to follow. Even stranger was his acceptance that Aaron could read his mind. Calmness had replaced his urgent need to identify his visitor. "Vibration is the secret of creation, you were saying," Sam initiated, picking up the conversation.

They now walked side by side, although Sam had found the path too narrow previously. "You say it is because of the nature of energy—more specifically of thoughts, as an expression of energy—everything has a frequency and, according to law, everything resonating on the same frequency is attracted?"

"When you strike a tuning fork, all other tuning forks calibrated to the same frequency will begin to vibrate, without your intervention. They begin to vibrate because they are of similar resonance, or are 'touched' by the same vibration. This principle is identical to my earlier example about strumming middle C on a piano."

"And this is the basis of thought energy."

"Right. Everything that exists was first a thought."

"And this is why consciousness and awareness are so vital. Without awareness, we let our minds run away with us. We remain mostly unaware of the stream of habitual, negative thoughts filling our minds."

"A stream of about seventy-five thousand thoughts, give or take, per day."

"And all of these thoughts carry frequencies—mostly negative due to our conditioning and past experiences."

"What a quick study you are, Sam!"

"I accept it because it is logical and makes so much sense. It is important to me that information makes sense, and is logical. I do not believe we live in an illogical universe."

"Your comment demonstrates your capacity for understanding. Remember that people do not question, much less comprehend a grain of what is beyond their grasp."

"This will be hard for others to believe."

"Belief in general is hard for people, Sam. So it is said, you must believe as a child."

"I don't think that adults can do it. I don't think they can believe as a child can."

"Why do you suppose that is?"

Sam thought about the answer. "Probably because of our negative conditioning and preconceived ideas of what is believable."

"And don't forget adults' insistence on proof. They look at their immediate world and claim it is real because they can see it, hear it, smell it, taste it, touch it. The test and the trap of the material world satisfy them."

"What is reality then?"

"What do you think, Sam? Can the realities of two people be identical?"

"No, because we create reality with our thoughts, and we all have different thoughts."

"That is correct. First, the thought exists, carried and underscored by the belief. Together these create your reality."

"This is another fundamental rule in the game, I think."

"You are correct again, Sam. Your beliefs create your reality because what you choose to believe comes from your thoughts. Everything you believe with conviction becomes part of your world; thus thought and belief are also interdependent."

"Aaron, this law sounds simple, but I don't think it is."

"You think it is complicated. Why?"

"I think that people don't examine their beliefs."

"Agreed, but why not?"

"It doesn't occur to them?"

"They do not examine their beliefs because they are unaware or unconscious."

"There is no softer way to say this?"

"If the child puts his hand on a hot plate, does the parent turn the temperature down so that it does not burn quite as much? Or does the parent say, 'Don't do it again!'?"

"Aaron, the entire human race behaves this way."

"You, Sam! We're not dealing with generalities tonight. It is not the human race; it is Sam. It is not their beliefs, but yours." Aaron dropped his voice. "The saying, 'According to your faith, let it be done unto you,' what does that mean?"

Sam smiled at the line of questioning. "It means that whatever you have faith in, you also believe. And what you believe, eventually happens." He quickly added, "With conviction, whatever beliefs I am certain of eventually come true."

"And? Do your beliefs come true?"

"Sometimes."

"If it happens only sometimes, Sam, it could not be a Law; it could not be a rule in the game."

"Aaron, it is not always easy to figure out our beliefs. Because we don't think about it all the time, it is possible that we don't even know what we believe!"

Aaron stopped to face him. "There is a very easy way to know, Sam. All you have to do is to look at your immediate world around you."

"Why? How will that help me?"

"Your beliefs are manifested in your world around you."

Sam contemplated that statement. "My beliefs are already in my world?" He looked at Aaron who didn't reply, but waited for Sam to see it.

When the silence began to stretch Aaron asked, "Tell me what you essentially believe about God."

"I honestly am not sure. I never knew if He was real or not. I wanted to believe that I could count on Him, but somehow I expected to be let down."

"You expected it?"

"Yes," Sam said hesitantly. Then with more conviction he added. "Yes! Yes, I expected to be let down. It's very hard to throw your lot in with a phantom."

Aaron laughed. "Can you see how beautifully the law works?"

They stood in the pathway facing each other. Low, swirling clouds surrounded them, ghostlike. "When you do not know if God is real, then your hope that He exists becomes a wish, nothing more. Now think about the saying we spoke of a minute ago, according to your belief, it is done unto you. If you do not know He is real, but you hope or wish He is, then what is your fundamental belief?"

"That He is not."

"Right," Aaron let out a pent-up sigh. "That's right. Do you still wonder why you expected to be let down? Through your most basic belief you invalidated the Being you thought, you hoped, could help you. You were expecting assistance from a God you did not give credence to; that assistance is therefore not possible! It is against the rules, Sam. You would surely be benched."

"Why would I be on the bench for this?"

"Anytime you want something, but feel you cannot obtain it, and then feel victimized, you directly influence how you see yourself and the world. Your model, remember, is reflected in your reaction to the world. Note, Sam, I say 'reaction,' not 'response.' When you react, in this case pay lip service to the existence of God, but expect that he does not exist, then your behavior comes from your conditioned self, not your real self."

"And belief and expectation go hand in hand?"

"Yes, they are as inseparable as thought and belief. It is impossible to believe one thing and expect the opposite to happen. You always get what you expect. And you get what you expect because you believe it."

"We are always creating our own worlds around us, is what you're saying."

"Always. The more conscious and aware you are, the better control you have of your life. You can steer your life if you learn how to direct your thoughts. That is what mastering your destiny means. It is learning how to work with the creative forces within you. Sam," Aaron said as he turned and started walking again, "belief is also the basis of what you call miracles."

For a while they walked together in silence. Then Sam said, "We have a popular idiomatic expression . . ."

"It is not valid." Aaron kept walking.

"Seeing is believing," Sam pressed on. "This concept is widely accepted in my culture."

"That does not make it either right or true. It comes from the New Testament story of Doubting Thomas. The axiom provides an excellent illustration of how unaware people can accept anything that sits easily on the tongue. They are not mindful of the power of the word. The word is powerful because it is the building block of thought, and thought has frequency; thus it communicates with the universe."

"The reverse therefore is true, before you see what you desire, you must believe it exists?" Sam ventured.

"Yes. If you insist on seeing, before believing, your expectation will deliver your doubt. You'll come away empty-handed every time."

Suddenly they reached the place where they had met the first time that night. The fog had lifted slightly and Sam recognized the edge of the cliff about twenty feet in front of him. Aaron sank down, in the same position, with his back against the same tree, where Sam had first seen him. He indicated another tree close by. "You will be comfortable there." Sam sat.

"In all the advanced cultures and religions, very clear guidelines are given to the people. Nobody is left stranded without a way to advance and grow. In your culture the guideline to understand the rule about Belief and Expectation is given in the analogy of the child." They were both sitting with their knees drawn halfway up, fingers linked together around their legs. "When you tell a child something exciting, what does she say to you?"

Sam knew Aaron expected no reply. He gave none.

"Does the child ask, 'Really, can I believe you?' Does the child ask, 'Where is the proof of the promise?'" Aaron smiled when he saw the expression in Sam's eyes.

"No. The little face lights up with expectation, asking 'when?' Do children not babble incessantly about their excitement, and are their expectations and joy not contagious as they bounce around with impatience? It is because they do not doubt the promise. They believe it completely, without reservation."

Sam could see Aaron's face clearly, despite the darkness, for a faint light came from the distant horizon.

"This unreserved belief carries enormously powerful energy. The universe reads a frequency like this as a clear communication. It does not emit the static of if or maybe, or show me proof. The message is untouched, candid and most of all, it is truthful."

"But children are not yet burdened by negative conditioning, Aaron," Sam said.

"That burden does not change the requirement! Your belief must be the belief of a child's—no ifs, ands, or buts.

"Miracle healings originate from the very same source. How beautiful your world is, if only you choose to see it! Your beliefs and expectations go hand in hand. You express these through your thoughts, words, and feelings, and, in turn, generate a frequency that communicates your deepest desires and dreams clearly to the universe. You cannot separate mind from body; they are one and the same. You cannot lie. Consequently," Aaron spoke more slowly, looking into Sam's eyes, "your body will perform miracles if you can believe like the child. Your body doesn't care about medical research; it follows where its master leads, as long as the master points the way."

"But people pray for others when they are very ill, and some do get better."

"What do you imagine causes the healing?"

In the silence that followed, even the night sounds were still.

Then Sam spoke out of certainty, "The sick people believed. They believed in the power of the person intervening on their behalf to a God they didn't think they could reach on their own. We have the power to perform miracles and it's hidden in belief. That is why the analogy of the mustard seed in the Christian Bible is so powerful. It is used to demonstrate how small our faith is."

"Indeed, Sam. You're right, how small the faith is, and how big the ego has become. Humans divide themselves into warring factions, killing each other over who owns the more reliable version of God and miracles. They fight among one another defending reports of people long dead, based on hearsay, on manuscripts delivered from antiquity. But most don't speak from personal experience."

Sam suddenly sat up, understanding dawning on his face. Aaron smiled. "Yes, Sam. Their egos are in the way. It is not about God; it is about them. They defend their beliefs because they cannot tolerate losing face. They cannot be wrong, and so their misdirected energy drags them into the very snare they set for all the 'unbelievers.' It is the snare of judging, the trap of conditional love leading to the inability to love their neighbor as they would themselves. While they point with one hand at the 'sinners,' they stretch the other hand to the sky, imploring forgiveness. All the gods laugh at that."

Sam inhaled every word, allowing it to fill every open space in his mind and body. "The backbone is belief, but prayer is an inner decision we make. I see that now, Aaron. If the mind is strong, it can make a decision on its own, and the body follows through. If the mind is weak, it can be influenced by the conviction of another, especially when the situation is difficult."

"Sam, the parameters of what is possible are set by you. That is law. Each person creates a force field around himself, establishing the limits of what can be. The force field reflects your energy ID, and your energy force field is your point of attraction.

"When a child is still open and trusting, adults provide the example. Initially, the child follows this example blindly. If the child later becomes aware and conscious, he will examine these parameters and decide for himself if those are still valid for him.

"If he does not become an independent thinker, the limits become walls. The person only lets in what he has already decided to believe. All else will be deemed 'wrong,' or, in the case of religion, sacrilegious. He will live in the same limited world and he will accept that as real and unchangeable."

"So our beliefs become blinkers that we wear?" Sam smiled at the mental picture of people dressed in elegant eveningwear, all with blinkers on their eyes, seeing only what their limited tunnel vision allowed them.

"Yes, tragic tunnel vision. When your most powerful tool of creation is forced into a narrow tunnel, how can you ever become more than you are? How can you see what is out there? How can you know the All?" Aaron rested his head against the trunk of the tree, and closed his eyes. When he spoke again, he sounded sad.

"Self-limiting beliefs have absolutely no basis in reality, Sam. They live only in your imagination. That is why an open mind is so important."

"But an open mind brings its own complexities. How can I know for certain what is right or wrong when I open myself to so many sources of information?"

"Sam, when you lift your consciousness above the level of the masses, you will understand that right and wrong do not exist. It exists, but only according to the level of consciousness you hold. That and only that, determines right from wrong. You learn very little about life and yourself when you have tunnel vision. You learn even less when you have already made up your mind that your ancestors had all the answers. Your growth will be stunted, and you'll live in their version of truth at the behest of your limited mind. And then you'll want to defend it."

"Why do people defend their beliefs with such vigor?"

"They need to be right." Aaron opened his eyes, but didn't look at Sam.

Sam leaned forward, his voice urgent. "Is it really possible for us to change our lives? If we are so conditioned, so trained in our responses, can we improve at all?"

Aaron closed his eyes again. He seemed lost in thought, but Sam knew he was paying close attention. "Earlier I said if you want to know your beliefs, examine your immediate environment. All your beliefs are manifested in your world."

"Yes, our beliefs create our worlds."

"So, if you look at that world of yours, and you decide it could stand some improvement, then all you have to do is to reverse the initial process."

"Change the belief?"

"Absolutely."

"That is easier said than done. Sorry, Aaron."

Aaron opened his eyes and looked at Sam. "Sorry? What are you sorry about?"

"Aaron," Sam was very serious, "much of what we have talked about tonight makes sense. I think I can learn to do a whole lot of new things, even make some changes. But I have had the privilege of meeting you on the mountain! What about the millions of people out there who do not have the benefit of talking to someone like you? How will they learn to change ingrained beliefs?"

Aaron nodded, equally serious. "So you are saying that other people are doomed. Their beliefs will chain them to lives of mediocrity and frustration. They will make the same mistakes over and over, with no possibility of effecting positive change?"

"I couldn't have said it better myself," Sam, now grinning, conceded.

"Throughout human history, we have many examples of people who were stuck one way or another, who stood up and cried, 'Enough!' "

"You're right; some have even written books."

"I did not meet them on a mountain. How did they do it?"

Sam considered his answer. "They wanted it, they really desired the way to make a change, I think."

"Yes, they wanted it, and they began to investigate the way. They discovered that beliefs are part of conditioning, and they discovered that they could transform their beliefs, when they worked hard enough at it.

"Ultimately, they discovered how powerful the mind is. They found that all behavior is motivated by the subconscious mind, and that the secret to programming is to gain entrance to this domain. They also discovered that the mind is your biggest ally—or your deadliest foe. And, Sam, they resolved to be friends with this power rather than take it on as an enemy." Aaron stood up. "They discovered more." He waited for Sam to stand also.

"Those who were really serious about their task discovered that the mind is the passageway leading to heaven, or to hell."

▲　▲　▲

Footprints, Fingerprints, and Clues

"Don't look down!" Aaron said firmly. They stood side by side, a footstep away from the abyss. Sam felt the cold mountain air at his back. From the gaping cliff in front of him, an even colder blast simultaneously blinded and beckoned him. The cliff's capacious mouth had been waiting the whole night, impatient to swallow him.

Sam's mouth had gone dry with panic, and the words stuck to his pallet when he tried to speak. "Why are we doing this?" It was a hoarse whisper, barely audible.

"Take your attention away from the precipice. Focus on the horizon."

Sam's every muscle was stretched and held in excruciating tension. His lungs were so constricted that he could only pant painfully.

"Open your eyes, Sam." Aaron was calm and firm. "Focus your attention on what you want, not on what you don't want."

"I don't want to be here!" Sam squeezed the words out in rasping terror.

"You are here. Now focus on the horizon," Aaron insisted. "Look there!" he said, pointing nonchalantly toward the horizon, "There is just the faintest promise of daybreak. The night will be over soon enough."

Sam opened his eyes slowly; tears streamed down his cheeks. He fought to bring the horizon into focus. "Oh my God."

"Sam, the subconscious mind is the sleeping giant," Aaron murmured soothingly.

They stood together still wrapped in darkness and faced the faint light starting its early morning dance across the water, where the curve of the ocean met the sky. "Its magnificent power is greatly underestimated."

Aaron gestured toward the light. He spoke in a soft tone, "Some claim the subconscious is the database that stores everything. It neither questions nor evaluates. It only accepts and keeps information. But, Sam, it is so much more, so much more."

"Please, Aaron, please." The nausea rose like a tidal wave, drowning everything but his terror. The abyss is drawing me. Imperceptibly, Sam leaned forward.

Aaron put his right arm out and held it straight across Sam's chest. He kept his eyes on the horizon. "It is so much more, Sam," he repeated. "It holds all your fears, your phobias, your darkest desires, and your dreams, your hopes, all your traits and talents, and your memories—including those you made today and yesterday—and," he laughed softly, still holding Sam securely in place with his arm, "those crafted in antiquity! All are held here, each and every one of them."

Sam's body remained rigid, but he focused on Aaron's voice. He needed to put something between him and the chasm of nothingness. He clung to every word, trying to make out the meaning.

"The subconscious holds both Pandora's box and a treasure chest." Together they stood silhouetted against the night sky. "But the gates are guarded by a ruthless taskmaster. You have to get past him, or all your efforts will be in vain. It will all come to naught." Aaron looked ahead, his eyes on the faint movement of light just below the ceiling of clouds arching toward the horizon.

"Who? Who is the gatekeeper? "Sam found his voice. He fixed his gaze on the horizon; his attention was seized by the puzzle. "The devil?"

"Bah! The devil again? Now there's a bloke who gets blamed for all we neither know nor understand." Aaron concentrated on the horizon. "No. This enemy is much closer to home. In fact, it grew up with you. First you trained it, and now it leads you by the nose. It lives with you moment to moment and you reinforce its power daily."

"Is it time for a riddle then?"

"Can you solve it, Sam? That's the question! Who is the gatekeeper?"

Sam felt the arm against his chest, holding him safely in place, as he focused all his attention on the puzzle.

Who was with him always? Who could it be? What dictated his behavior? They had started talking about the mind. Aaron's style of communication is to lead one to discover answers. Aaron is not in the habit of . . . Sam drew his breath in slowly, "I know who it is," he said calmly. "It is habit. Habit is the gatekeeper."

Aaron didn't reply. The silence stretched out and for a moment Sam thought he had it wrong, but then he heard the chuckle next to him and turned his head to look. Aaron's whole body was shaking as he laughed. Sam started smiling too, the spectacle was quite comical. There they were, standing on the edge of the cliff, two men dangerously perched on the rim of the world, laughing.

"Tonight you have not disappointed me, Sam," Aaron said through his laughter. "You see how everything opens up when you drop the fetters of false consciousness?"

"The what?"

"When you pretend to know, when you don't, or when you pretend not to know, when you do."

"Is this the same as lying to oneself?"

"It is more like fooling oneself. It is the same as complaining that you're kept in the dark, when you have your hand on the light switch. It all goes back to the thinking process again. Life can be very simple, if you are vigilant enough to notice the clues."

"What clues? You were talking about the subconscious mind. And I am still waiting to hear about Pandora's box and the treasure chest!"

"And you will, you will. Although, you already know."

"Habit is the gatekeeper." Sam ruminated. "Meaning we go over the same things in our minds, and revisit memories or events, and behave in certain ways, and we do so through habit or conditioning.

"We can wrest the key to the treasure chest from Habit, if we are able to stay conscious and aware. Then we direct our thoughts and change behaviors through choice. Or we sit by Pandora's box regurgitating everything negative and unhappy. And if we do, then we always come across more unwanted items that tear our hearts out, scare us, and make us miserable. And this happens because we are not conscious enough to see that Habit is leading us there; that we taught it to do so?"

"Yes, Sam. The subconscious mind is the sleeping giant because its power is so magnificent. Its close ally is Habit. The more aware you become, the better you understand the power of Habit. It is possible to reprogram your subconscious mind and there are many examples of successful people who learned how to do this. Affirmations work best when there is a conscious, alert mind behind the programming."

"But we are told that if we repeat positive statements regularly, whether we believe them or not, it eventually will deliver the desired outcome," Sam said, but as he spoke the words he saw the error in the reasoning.

Aaron acknowledged the mistake and Sam's recognition of it in silence.

"So," Sam said, lifting his hand to move Aaron's arm from across his chest, and turning to face him, "it is the feeling that counts. If we cannot repeat an affirmation with feeling it means we do not believe it. The energy ID would be equal to that of an unbeliever, and we cannot have what is impossible to believe, however positive and noble it sounds."

Both men relaxed into their customary listening postures, arms crossed over the chest. To one side of them, the flat surface of the mountain stretched far into the night, and then dipped down into the valley below to meet the vineyards of the Cape Province. From here, more mountains carved their way through forests, rivers, and deserts to delineate the continent of Africa. And below him was that incredible abyss, but Sam no longer felt the fear of being drawn toward it.

He stared at Aaron. "And the language of the universe is energy. It knows what we believe by taking our fingerprint." He stuck his finger in his mouth and then brought it out, pretending to make an imprint in the cold, white air in front of him. "And then the universe brings to us exactly what we call for. It does not listen to the deception of our words when we say one thing but intend another, but reads what we are."

Aaron stood quite still, watching while Sam thought, then formulated his words carefully and reached for deeper understanding, stretching the intellect and opening pathways to deeper insights.

Aaron spoke softly, "If you can recognize the clues that have been left here and have patience to follow the footprints, you will understand things that others for millennia have fought about. And still kill for. They give it all manner of names, but really they are asking, who am I, and what is my purpose here? You do not discover your purpose without knowing who you are. It is possible to understand things externally, but nothing is integrated without inner verification. And inner verification is the source of all knowledge; it opens the door to understanding eternity. It is the way of creation and the reason why all change must come along this path. The way of coming into being is always inside out."

Sam's eyes shone with excitement and unshed tears. "Clues are everywhere in nature, and in our immediate environment. Finger-prints are within us, identifying us, and revealing who we are. A foot-print is an inner understanding, a certain knowledge that brings us closer to the hem of the white robe that silently disappeared around the next corner. It is what we follow and can become."

Aaron spoke reverently, "The way of God, and to God, is to know you first. Always."

Sam nodded, feeling the energy course through him. "Everything works in interdependent unity and has a purpose."

"Everything," Aaron echoed. "There are no coincidences and no mistakes. Nobody rolls a dice. The sleeping giant—the subconscious mind—is an inseparable energy source with the conscious mind and universal mind. It is pure folly for man to imagine that he is separate from the whole, for it simply cannot be. There is only one mind, but people are free to plead ignorance and to take their own time to work their way to higher understanding through the trials and tribulations they create for themselves. They are also free to fool themselves and pretend they never knew. But if they find even a single footprint, and understand that they make their own destiny, they will look for another."

"Mind, body, and spirit, they are the same being—me. That is a footprint?" Sam felt the excitement of a breakthrough. "But what about . . .?" He froze, unable to voice it. A wilderness of a whole other kind stretched out in front of Sam as he considered what he had just encountered. They looked at each other. Sam trembled.

"Say it, Sam. Why do you shy away from it?" Aaron asked, calmly.

"Habit, I suppose." He laughed nervously. "How powerful habit is!" He hesitated, "You know what I am thinking. Is it not blasphemous, Aaron?"

"This is the footprint that almost everyone misses." He said it quietly.

Then Sam knew it. There was no mistaking his feelings; it was a clear knowing that brooked no argument. It came from his center, and it was a knowing that was unadulterated and pure. "Father, Son, and Holy Ghost are an integral part of humanity," he said deliberately. "Mind, body, spirit—Father, Son, Holy Ghost!" he repeated. "It makes so much sense. But for as long as we sleep, these are the aspects of ourselves that keep us hidden from ourselves." As he said the words, an immense weight lifted from him. He felt as if he were floating, and he wanted to laugh aloud. Instead, his face contorted with an incomprehensible emotion. He covered his ears with his hands, an involuntary defensive action from his childhood. He screamed silently.

Aaron slowly nodded his confirmation. "Yes, Sam." His voice dropped to a low whisper. "Yes, Sam. All scriptures confirm the birth of God in man. You cross an immense chasm of fear when you first consider the truth of that statement, just as you hesitated when you recognized it tonight. Few are equipped to venture across this wasteland. Few can navigate this quagmire fraught with past conditioning, religious dogmas, terrible fears, popular beliefs, pressures, and societal expectations. But comprehension and true insight wait on the other side. You have to take that first step—now, or in another life. Those who cannot pass are not yet free enough."

"What does that mean?"

"You tell me."

Sam turned away to face the abyss. Fog and mist swirled gently, as though an invisible hand were stirring it from above. He marveled that he no longer feared the great drop below him. How had he overcome his fear? He knew he would understand later.

He remembered the Hindu legend he had read years ago. The gods decided to hide the godhead deep within man because they knew that was the one place where man would never think to look. The story had meant nothing to him then. He had still been camping around the fires of experts who said God was in heaven out there, somewhere. He lifted his eyes and tried to scan the heavens, hidden from sight by the low clouds and the swirling fog.

He remembered how as a child, he had often tried to picture that promised place in the sky. Somehow, it always eluded him as if a deeper, hidden intelligence protected him from such fantasies. He scanned the scene in front of him, while an unfathomable lightness came over him. Then he knew why so few crossed that final wasteland. "They are not free enough because they do not truly think for themselves. They let others do their thinking for them. They rely on the credentials of agents."

Aaron hid the quick smile and gave Sam a quizzical look.

"Yes," Sam's voice held sadness—the voice of one who had traveled down that road many times and always returned empty-handed, "the ministers, priests, and the learned people who claim to be experts. Unaware man doesn't realize that another cannot accept responsibility for his life. And this alone has to blind him to original discoveries."

"It blinds him to truth." Aaron continued with Sam's thought. "Many millions wait to be saved at the gates of hell. They have been led there by the experts. Truth cannot be taught; it must be discovered. It is never secondhand, and it is not for sale. Even when you are told a truth, you must experience it before you will own it.

"The difference between authentic and forged knowledge is apparent to the keen observer. He notices it in the eyes of the deceiver and reads it in body movement, but most of all, intuitively he cannot be fooled. He knows. The mind is the mediator that keeps you in misery or unlocks all the wonders of this world. It is the most powerful creative tool of man. And it is the ticket to 'eternity' or to 'hell.'

"If a person does not learn how to temper this power, or understand it, he or she lives by their own decree, unconscious as it might be, in changeable but continuous states of depression. Depression is the result of extreme victimhood and self-pity. It is to be without God, not to know yourself, and that is hell.

"Or a person cracks the shell of the egg, and lets in the Light. This is the point where mind steps back altogether and allows Spirit to lead the rest of the way. Freedom ceases to be a fantasy and transforms into reality for the first time when we discover heaven is within, not without.

"We grasp truth when we understand that everything relates to a state of consciousness. Such a state is a degree of understanding that supersedes words, or the frustrated cries of the crowds who have not yet found themselves. Your journey in this world does not truly start until you recognize that you create it all. Then, and only then, do you learn the Rules of the Game and can you play. The Rules of the Game are the guidelines that help you understand how to play the game. And, Sam, there is no degree to truth. All the teachers and prophets taught the same rules. Truth is the Law of Life. And that law is self-learned.

"'Heaven' is not an option for those who are trying to escape what they have created but refuse to deal with. They want forgiveness and expect mercy. Even after what is known as death, the laws operate, and people swiftly find themselves back at the starting line, with a chance to do it again. That is the real meaning of mercy."

"Mind rules the body and opens doors to higher understanding," Sam said, "in direct proportion to our levels of consciousness and understanding. And this means we can skip over what is possible or impossible, the true limitations of the material world. Possibility always depends on the faith of the one who poses the question. The free human being knows that if the mind can conceive an idea and believe it with feeling, the universe delivers. It does so not through coincidence, but by law."

"Some call it mental magic," Aaron said, "but if you could step aside from your material body you would witness the wonder of how creation comes about. The masses not only believe in limitation, they worship it, and you have to overcome their terrible nagging and their angry taunts. If you want to grow, you must be prepared to walk alone. They will accuse you of playing God, avoid you, and disdain you. And while they judge you, in the very same breath they will confess their sins and helplessness.

"They don't see the quicksand of the accusation that they are the ones playing God. And always, always they keep an eye on heaven's door wondering when it will open and let them into eternal bliss. The contradiction between their behavior—what they are and what they expect as a final outcome—is completely lost to them. They break a fundamental rule of the game and then wonder why they feel so miserable, depressed, and unfulfilled."

Listening to the quiet, even voice Sam wondered at how much Aaron and he sounded alike, especially when he, Sam, was calm and at peace. He watched the play of light become stronger and stronger as it flashed along the horizon, imitating muffled lightening activity behind clouds. The night was not yet ready to relinquish her hold on this side of earth, but she was opening her fist ever so slightly to let in tiny streaks of day. Her reign was temporary and she knew it.

"You speak of The Law of Correspondence," Sam smiled. "The inside-out approach. That must be why it is so important for us to know ourselves, and why it is so clearly demonstrated as a principle in all cultures and religions."

"The only way you will ever learn about yourself is to observe yourself." Aaron continued in Sam's voice. "You have to watch your behavior, notice when you lose control, or when your reactions are conditioned, learned responses that come from your mechanical self—the part that does not think.

"When you feel hurt by the comments or behaviors of others, you have to be conscious enough to stop and ask yourself, why did I allow this to happen? Why am I feeling this way? What hurts me, their words, or my reaction to their words? Is it possible for another to hurt me without my permission? What weighs more, their words or my knowing?

"Honest self-examination and inquiry will lead you to deeper insight and understanding. Self-discovery, knowing thyself, does not come about without this. The opinion of another becomes insignificant when you comprehend that the human being has to overcome his self-absorption first before he cares about you. Everything others tell you is their perspective. And their perspective is flawed, tainted, or enriched by their life experiences to the exact degree that they have the ability to look within and then face the person in the mirror.

"If a person cannot be honest with himself, or herself, how does their opinion benefit you, except on the surface? Who looks into your heart and feels your pain, or knows your bliss? If you discover something of value, are others of lesser understanding excited when you share your knowledge and insights with them? No, they cannot be. Their self-absorption drives them to compete. They are consumed with their own selves. They compare what you say to what they have; they see the difference, and the distance is already created. Not by you, but by them. That is the nature of the unconscious person."

"And this is the secret to self-development and growth." Sam added. "If we can catch ourselves in our moments of deep hurt, uncontrolled anger, and darkest depression, we confront Habit. There is no other way to change negative behavior patterns or habits other than to stop doing things the way we did them before. The mold has to be broken." Sam could hardly contain himself.

Aaron smiled. "Yes, Sam. Until you learn this, Habit stands at the gate and yells with the might and force of millennia's conditioning, "You will not pass! You cannot get by me!'"

"So our conditioned, unconscious behavior comes from the sub-conscious mind, which rules everything unless we become conscious, aware, and wake up to ourselves. Habit stands aside when we begin to choose our responses, and that only happens when we take conscious control of the content of our conscious minds," Sam marveled at the ease with which Aaron and he spoke together, finishing each other's sentences. "When you teach the conscious mind new pathways, new responses, it will take you past the gatekeeper. The sleeping giant will wake and will lead you to a treasure chest of new experiences and choices."

"Oh yes, Sam. It will show you how to master the body, under-stand destiny, and open a doorway to one, universal mind. Then it will take you to Spirit and bow out. And then you'll see another clue; get an inkling of where to look for yet another footprint."

They looked together at the far horizon. Night had finally con-ceded defeat. The tentative shadow-dance of light had been replaced by a pencil-thin line of dawn. In time, daybreak would birth the sun and send it floating briefly across the water in a golden path of prom-ise of the day ahead, then lift it into the blue sky.

Sam thought in wonder about the magnificence of mind, how powerful it was to bring forth exactly what he feared or loved. He thought about the power of belief, and how mind depends on belief to reveal its real potential. He thought about God. Aaron had said that they were not talking about God tonight, but the topic seemed impossible to avoid. He thought about the kingdom of God within. In a few brief moments, a lifetime of searching and questioning flowed through him. *How could I be in the presence of the Creator if my own being cannot stand the pure vibration of untainted, complete belief?* It felt so impossible.

"The answer is in forgiveness, Sam. That is the next fingerprint you're looking for." They turned to face each other again. "When you learn to forgive yourself for all your imperfections, you'll also see that all is One. Forgiveness is the key to gaining momentum in your forward movement. Nothing can be separate from the whole. The whole is not only what you see here and now. Your world is the first of many, but you must master this one first. But you will not do that without gifting the gift of forgiveness."

▲　▲　▲

Gifting Forgiveness

"Tell me about Karla." They were sitting at the edge of the cliff watching the daylight take over the world by degrees. Sam lay down on his back; knees bent slightly, his hands cupped beneath his head. He watched the slow-moving clouds drift above him, ushering in the day. The lady of the mountain was slowly undoing her cloak.

Then he closed his eyes and Karla was before him. His body tensed, tormented by the familiarity of her and the distance between them. Karla.

Aaron chewed on a long piece of grass as he watched the play of emotion on Sam's face. He settled down to wait.

"I loved her before I met her," Sam said simply.

"I know," Aaron replied. "You were both very young."

Sam seemed unaware that Aaron had spoken. "I think the idea of her was always in me somewhere, a dream or a vision of some kind." He let the memories flood in. "I modeled the image of her on pure fantasy, you know." He opened his eyes and stared at an invisible spot above him in the clouds. "I had nothing to imagine her on, except a faint hope, a feeling that some day . . ." Sam closed his eyes. Aaron waited.

"I struggled relating to women early in my life," he said when he had regained his composure. "I desperately tried to bridge the void between my father and me with something or someone, so I turned to the women I knew. I needed them to be warm, soft, and sympathetic, but it never happened. It just wasn't there. I told you about my mother and the sister I hardly knew." He opened his eyes. "My parents' marriage was not loving or harmonious, but I clung to the hope that it could be different for me. On some level I might even have deliberately excluded them from my life."

Aaron nodded imperceptibly.

"I was so anxious for it to be different that I cultivated the dream until I came to believe my own fantasies. Of course now I understand that it had to happen because I believed it so!"

Sam looked at Aaron without seeing him. "We moved into the neighborhood when I was sixteen. At sixteen, I was neither worldly nor experienced. But years of solitude had trained my mind to consider possibilities that intrigued and excited my body, kept in check only by lack of confidence. My desires stayed fantasies. Then we were invited to their house."

He closed his eyes briefly, wonder in his voice. "The moment she stepped into the room, she took my breath away."

Aaron smiled gently in acknowledgment.

"She was only twelve, a little waif hanging around alone in a grownup world with seemingly nowhere else to go. It was as if we had been waiting for each other." Sam felt grateful for the companionable silence.

Finally, Aaron spoke, "She is an only child and you were almost like one; you were both lonely children. But loneliness is a scheming, tough matchmaker that sometimes bonds people through despair. Is that what happened?"

Sam didn't respond. *Despair? Oh no, not despair.*

He was back in the living room of her parents' house, looking out from his corner when she skipped barefoot into the room. She had been called from outside, and her face shone with the glow of the hot, summer sun.

He stared at the beautiful, tiny creature standing beside her mother, and his heart missed a beat. He saw the long, dark hair, untidily caught in a ponytail reaching down to the middle of her back. Her little hand kept brushing loose strands of hair from her eyes as she spoke to her mother in subdued tones. When she turned to him, his mouth went dry. He saw the big, gray eyes under the neatly curved eyebrows; the straight little nose perched determinedly above a wide mouth that laughed easily.

"Oh!" Her eyes widened as she formed the perfect vowel and drew her breath in. "You're Sam! I know about you. At school . . ." She caught herself, just a tiny child-woman; but she was not about to give up her secrets. Then she held out her hand to him as if it were the most natural thing for a sixteen-year-old boy to take the hand of a twelve-year-old wisp of a thing and be led out of the room in front of their parents. He got up, but didn't take the outstretched hand, and followed her down the corridor through the kitchen, leading to the huge backyard.

"We have pigeons—homing pigeons," she explained. "And we fly them!" she finished proudly. She looked over her shoulder to make sure he was following.

Sam was mesmerized by the innocence of her as she moved in front of him, a bewildering collage of child and woman; her hips moving rhythmically between the skips and jumps. His emotions were a mystery to him. He roller-coasted along between his need to control the situation and his attraction to the chatter of this nymph-like figure leading the way. When they emerged from the dark house into the sunshine she suddenly broke into a run, her hair flying in the wind, catching the sunlight. She ran toward a wood and wire structure at the far end of the garden.

Sam stood in the blazing hot sun and watched her dart away, an unfamiliar happiness squeezing his heart, making it race uncontrollably. He felt joy being in her presence, sharing a mysterious familiarity when she called his name as if they had known each other forever.

"Come on, Sam! Two of them are going to have babies!" she pointed excitedly to the big cage, giggling, waiting with dancing eyes for him to catch up.

He hesitated, trying to locate the source of the joy. And suddenly he knew! He had not hoped in vain! His heart knew the beautiful creature waiting at the birdcage; she had stepped out of his dreams and into the real world, his world.

She looked up at him as he approached, her face filled with the pleasure of sharing her prized possessions. "My dad says these birds are magical," she beamed. "They always find their way home. No matter how far we take them, they always come back to us!"

Although still a child, Sam knew she was feminine and soft. She'd never compete with the boys; she'd let them win—that way she couldn't lose! The softness was in her playful laugh, and the woman modestly veiled in those beautiful wide, gray eyes. When she grew older, she would be warm and loving. Oh God! His heart stopped for a painful moment as he considered the revelation. He was only sixteen and his dream stood in front of him! Was it too soon? How would he keep it to himself and for so long? She was barely a teenager.

He was afraid that he would cry but he didn't, and he swallowed hard. He wanted to embrace her, press her to his heart, but he simply stood and looked at her. "Which ones are going to have babies, Karla?" he asked, shakily, her laugh echoing in his ears. Everywhere he looked he saw her eyes. Karla. His Karla, who now had shut him out completely.

"What could you not forgive her? What devastated you so much that you could not reach out to catch her when she started falling?"

Sam forced his memory back. She too, was scarred, but she found ways to hide her wounds better. Unlike his quiet, almost brooding exterior, she laughed a lot and was openly inquisitive, a seemingly carefree child. But she too was weighed down by the loneliness and manipulation of a mother who had suffered multiple miscarriages—a mother who smothered her only child. She claimed ownership of the little girl and never let Karla forget how much she had suffered, how hard it was to be a woman. In time, she burdened her only child with the guilt of the 'one who made it.' Oblivious to the damage she had done, she did not notice when Karla began to dread walking down the same road someday.

Karla and he became close friends. They had married, a natural transition, when she turned twenty-four. But before her thirtieth birthday she had miscarried twice. She was convinced she was incapable of carrying a baby full term. The anxiety and stress of childbearing—learned from her mother—was firmly established, and he watched helplessly as despair swept her away. Sam withdrew to what he knew, the example of withdrawal set by his mother. He had no idea how to comfort or reassure Karla.

Uncomfortably each tried to fill the other's hollow spaces, tried to ignore the childhood shadows of insecurity that followed them around everywhere. Early in their marriage, they had waited for each other to emerge from the dark recesses of their minds, when the world overpowered them. Unaware of choice making, they let the waiting periods became commonplace. Both practiced a special kind of avoidance that did not draw them closer or help to resolve conflict, but accentuated the differences. Despite their deep love for one another, they reflected each other's shortcomings—opening a deep chasm between them. Into this chasm Sam would disappear, silent for days on end, leaving her to fend for herself.

The childhood dream struggled to stay alive, reflected sometimes in a fleeting look, a passing memory. They had begun to repeat the patterns they had learned so well from their parents.

He felt entitled to this beautiful woman whom he had claimed for himself when she was only twelve. He expected her to know his deepest feelings, which he could not share. She didn't understand, and the distance increased. Karla saw her childhood hero become a distant stranger, who had abandoned her to shoulder loss and pain alone. She couldn't; and the baby's death was the catalyst for the end of their relationship. He forced his mind to revisit those dark corners where the terrible silence between them overpowered their best intentions, and blame became their only defense.

"I hated the fact that she was so sick during the pregnancy." Sam sat up and looped his arms around his knees. Aaron listened.

"I now know how selfish it was, but I couldn't escape the thought that she had let us both down. I couldn't forgive her for allowing that beautiful promise of our childhood meeting to go to ruin. I couldn't accept the death of my dream and I blamed her for it.

"I agonized over why her perfect, healthy body could not sustain another life successfully. Where was the flaw? That thought drove me crazy. I saw how miserable and anxious that made her, but I was powerless to overcome my own insecurities, much less to help her. I thought that a love like ours was destined to succeed, and I couldn't believe what was happening. I had no idea of how much work a good relationship required, and I was too immature to admit my own shortcomings. The disappointment was so intense we had to deflect it on one another. I was caught up in my own struggles with insignificance. How could I help her, or anybody, when I was not equipped to take care of myself?

"She became convinced she had failed as a woman and I did nothing to correct that terrible thought. If anyone knew how much of a woman she was, I did. We had waited eight years for our daughter, and when she died we both experienced a death of another kind—the worst kind—because paradoxically it lets you live. It allows you to breathe, but without mutual support it slowly sucks the life from you until you can find no reason to continue and you give in, like Karla did, or you find a mountain, like I did."

"It does not have to be over," Aaron spoke slowly and deliberately. "That is still up to both of you. The circumstances do not determine the final outcome, Sam. Emotional maturity is much more significant." He smiled a crooked smile. "With all their technological and intellectual progress, humans remain emotionally stunted. They fail to understand that they imprison themselves with guilt, hatred, and blame. In this prison they are free to act out their victimhood for as long as it takes their consciousness to see that the misery is of their own making. And to understand that it will continue for as long as they refuse to forgive others, and themselves. The negative emotion holds you in bondage. You can forgive her, and ask her to forgive you. Have you considered that option?"

"I'd do anything . . ."

"Don't say that if you're not prepared to follow through, Sam."

Sam was taken aback by his brusqueness. "Aaron, I have learned so much. I am willing to do anything to rescue the relationship, to go back and start again."

"If you are serious, then you had better start with yourself. You must start with yourself because you need to be free."

"From what, Aaron?"

"Most people assume they love themselves. They don't, but they put on a convincing performance. Without self-love, you will never find inner peace. You will never be able to share inner peace with another because you cannot give what you don't have. The 'gates of heaven' will not open and no amount of praying will accomplish that miracle either." Aaron smiled. "A fundamental rule in the game, as we have discussed, is the inside-out approach!

"The rules are not bent for anyone; there is no other way! Before you can bring another peace, or forgive them, you have to give yourself that gift. You are the first recipient of your own forgiveness and love. All attempts to reverse this process are just hollow words that nobody believes.

"When you forgive yourself, you will know what honoring yourself means. Only then do you have any hope of finding the divine spark within. And when you do, you will know why 'forgiveness is divine.' Forgiving yourself or another is the act that finally sets you free." Aaron looked Sam in the eye, unwavering "And that is nothing short of godliness."

"Forgiving is not conditional." Sam meant it as a question, but it came out as a statement.

"How can it be, Sam? 'If' sets the condition and reveals the intent as weak and self-centered. 'If' kills the intent of the forgiving. And intent is the foundation of creation."

"I don't understand that." Sam frowned.

"Intent is driven by emotion, and emotion is the fuel of creation. Emotion carries your energy fingerprint and the universe does not, cannot mistake it. Subconsciously others read that also, that is why like attracts like." Aaron had a twinkle in his eye. "Sam, when the gods hear 'if' as you grant your forgiveness to another, they turn on their heels and walk away! They know you have simply found another way to manipulate others into having it your way, that you are striking a bargain and that you will remember their transgressions soon enough. You will lay the same offense, for which you forgave them yesterday, before their feet tomorrow and ask: "Have you forgotten my pain?"

Sam was silent.

He thought about Karla and how much he wanted to share this information with her. He ached all over. He wanted to hold her in his arms and tell her how sorry he was for all the hurt and the pain, the lack of communication and understanding. He wanted to apologize for being so self-centered that he couldn't be there for her, and he wanted to make up for it. He wanted to relieve her from the terrible burden of guilt and remorse that gripped her so viciously that it put her in a hospital and was squeezing the life out of her. He closed his eyes; he couldn't bear the thought of her suffering.

"Before you go to her, you have to come to yourself," Aaron said evenly. "Do you understand that, Sam?"

"Yes, I think so." Sam spoke softly, his eyes on the far horizon where the day edged in closer. "I have to forgive myself for all the self-hate, all the terrible fears and devastating anger, all the insignificance I felt all of these years because I didn't really know myself. Most of all, I have to forgive myself for howling from my own prison cell when all the time the lock was on the inside, and the key was in my hand, in my heart. Only then can I ask forgiveness of all whose lives I made unbearable by blaming them for my misery.

"Karla will never have me back conditionally, if she'll have me, Aaron," his voice grew stronger. "I know that I can never go to her as I was before. She will see immediately."

"Yes, Sam, Karla will see. She will know. That's why she would not see you yesterday. Nothing had changed. But Karla will know because she knows your heart, and the heart doesn't lie. It is incapable of doing so.

"All humans know—but they trick themselves into believing they don't—opting this way for a life that is second rate at best. When people lie, the eyes and heart have no part in it. It is not hard to tell when someone is treading the path of deception."

"Aaron, Karla is so depressed. Will she be able to tell that I am different?"

Aaron smiled, his eyes scanning the faint pink color showing where the ocean dropped off at the end of the earth. "Karla will know because she loves you. She'll know because forgiveness comes directly from the heart. The heart does not consult the intellect, nor is it known for its reasoning ability. Forgiving is a gift because it comes from the heart. The real gift is the heart, Sam, and you captured hers years ago at the birdcage, remember?

"The heart listens to words but is guided by emotion and feeling. Even if you are not eloquent, the heart still knows. Her heart will know."

"You said that we are held in bondage by negative emotion."

"Yes."

"When we carry grudges we literally hide from healing." He didn't wait for Aaron's response. "If everything is an expression of energy, then negative emotions are very powerful because of the compounded feelings behind them. Feelings convert into frequencies which build force fields around us, and ultimately that is our energy fingerprint. When we carry grudges, our attention is on the problem or wrongdoing, which by law means that we will be attracting more of the same experiences or events into our lives."

"Why, Sam! I don't think I could have said it any better. Consciousness and awareness. That is why it is so important! The more aware you become, the clearer your options are, and the less important it is to win. When winning no longer consumes you, negative emotion begins to lose its power over you. There is really only one question to consider: Do you want to be happy or do you want to be right?" With this they both burst out laughing. Sam was surprised at the joyful transformation on the face of this otherwise serious man.

"That's really it, isn't it, Aaron?" Sam asked when the laughing subsided.

"Our insistence upon being right binds us to the grindstone of laboring the point until we either win or die. Some would rather die than be wrong." Sam shook his head in disbelief. "My God, how could I not have seen this before? All negative emotion, refusal to forgive nails us to one spot. It holds us back but we do not see it.

"We cannot see it when we insist upon being right! Negative emotion is extremely powerful because it multiplies the control of the person whom you hate or dislike. You hand your control over, begrudgingly no doubt, but you do!" Sam looked at Aaron incredulously, "It has to be so! Just the thought of someone you dislike has the power to send you into a tailspin and puts your emotions instantly out of control. Even if they are a thousand miles away they control your feelings without them knowing it! The only trigger you need is the negative emotion, the grudge, the inability to let go, or to forgive . . ." Sam's voice trailed off as he began to understand the full implication of the difficulty so many people struggle with. "There is not a lot of hope for the human race is there, Aaron?" He sounded despondent.

"On the contrary, nothing stops them from coming to their senses. Nothing but them. Holding on to grudges and past grievances keeps you from moving forward. When you take steps to move forward, you're living, but if you decide to hold on to the past, death is certain. The first death is mental and emotional, and then the body will yield its life force. It always follows mind. The issue is one of choice. And the choice to let go of the past leads to superior mental health, a state many claim to have, but show scant evidence of."

Sam was silent again. So much of what had been discussed he needed to integrate, and there was still so much more he wanted to know. He didn't want the night to end before he had the chance to ask all the questions filling his mind. He thought about the concept of superior mental health. He thought about the mental anguish of so many people; a condition accepted as normal for the race. He thought about the terrible torment the mind inflicts upon an unaware person, and how difficult it is to escape from a condition of which you are not aware. Then he thought of Karla, and in that very moment her dilemma was clear to him. And he understood.

Sam closed his eyes, trying to shut out the vision of her. He saw how the remorse she felt for their dead child, their failed marriage drove her into that hospital, and he felt the spasm in his chest as his heart physically registered the pain of losing her. Her inability to forgive herself kept the door on healing firmly shut. It made her an emotional cripple dependent on chemicals to provide a break from the dreadful, overwhelming internal pressures, threatening her sanity. She was so alone in this struggle! His heart ached as he thought of her, and his mouth went dry as his mind swiftly transported him back to their childhood. They were standing at the birdcage in that blazing hot sun. Her tiny body was on tiptoe reaching up to identify the 'ones having babies.'

"You'll have to pick me up. I can't see from here, Sam!" she implored. "Lift me just a little please?" She was a very young twelve and he, a bewildered sixteen. With her back to him she lifted her arms and looked expectantly over her shoulder, eager to show off her feathered treasure to him.

Sam bent his already tall frame and put his one arm around her girlish, straight waist and lifted her easily off the ground just high enough to see the birds nesting at the very back of the cage in the cool shade.

"There!" She shrieked with pleasure pointing her finger to the beady black eyes of the pigeons that seemed oblivious to the activity at the front of the cage. They did not appear nearly as glad to see her. Sam hardly looked at the birds. She had turned her head to see his reaction, and her ponytail was in his eyes, in his mouth. He smelled fresh apple shampoo in her hair with just a trace of sweat from the summer heat, and he liked it. He wanted to put his other hand up and stroke the shiny dark hair, and it scared him. He put her down quickly.

"Jesus Christ . . ." he whispered hoarsely, lifting an arm to wipe away a stray tear.

"Don't do that, Sam." He felt the hand briefly squeeze his shoulder. "That is the very same trap she is caught in. When you try to understand a loss by projecting it on a beautiful memory the disparity is too big, and the pain very hard to handle. The contrast alone is powerful enough to destroy the memory, making it bitter. Then you will remember the bitterness and forget the joy."

Aaron paused briefly. "When you feel such deep sorrow, self-pity tends to show its ugly head. Self-pity is self-absorption dressed in its most deceptive garment for it comes to you as your pain, and who can refuse it entry? And do you not feel entitled to your pain? Unfortunately it doesn't end there. When self-pity transforms into remorse, well, that is when forgiveness almost equals a miracle. It is very hard to do because you have to get past yourself first."

Sam sat motionless thinking about how much forgiving he needed to do. He was aware of a lightness in his chest but where Karla was concerned, he was uncertain. He looked at Aaron. "Tell me how! I feel as though I should know the answers but when I think about it, my mind goes blank. I cannot lose her, I don't want to. Not after tonight. There is so much living still to do, but it includes her. How do I do it, Aaron? I think I am going to need a miracle, please help me!"

"You need a miracle, Sam?" Aaron chuckled. "I thought you knew I didn't do them. Was I mistaken?" Seeing the expression on Sam's face he leaned over as if to share a secret. "You don't need a miracle, Sam. But you can learn a lesson or two from the magical birds."

Sam stared at him. "What?"

Aaron ignored the incredulous overtone. "By the way, did you ever get to see the babies?"

Sam was exasperated. "The birds? Aaron, what are you talking about . . .?"

He was unperturbed. "Yes, Sam. Karla's magical birds. Isn't it ironic that your relationship began there? Only, you did not get the symbolism or understand the meaning then."

Sam relaxed and sat back. "Tell me, Aaron. I know you want to."

Aaron smiled. "Homing pigeons and humans have something extraordinary in common shared by no other creatures on the planet in quite the same way." He glanced over at Sam and then turned his gaze to the skies as if looking to spot one flying up there.

"Both the human being and homing pigeon have a natural homing system. The bird instinctively flies home because its goal is to return home. Its inner direction never fails because it is its natural state. Humans have the same ability but it is not instinctive, it has to be cultivated.

"Man becomes frustrated and unhappy when he lacks inner direction, and lacking inner direction is the same as failing yourself. It is not unlike a bird that never takes off and always has to eat off the ground.

"You have to set course in every aspect of your life. The bird does so automatically but you have to work at it. Without a clear focus you are simply stumbling from day to day. The bird always knows where it is going but you have to find out, determine where you'd like to go.

"Once you have clarity about what you want to accomplish and why, you'll fly straight home to her if that is what you still want. And you will in every respect surpass the bird in magnificence."

▲ ▲ ▲

Fill Up On Your Dream

"So, there is no one to blame," Sam said, stretching his legs as he got up from the grass. He peered briefly over the edge of the cliff and winced. "I don't know that I will ever be rock climbing, but the fear has left me." He smiled and looked over at Aaron, leaning against the trunk of a tree with folded arms, waiting. "We're going back?"

Aaron nodded, turning to head up the hill leading to the restaurant. Sam fell into step behind him. Much of their conversation had taken place as they walked along the paths on the flat surface of this mountain; they were back at it again.

"You're right about not laying blame at another's door, yet the world teems with unhappy people. Why is that, Sam? What cross do they bear?"

Sam's mind was elsewhere. He thought about Karla's magical pigeons and he felt his heart warm. To this day she has a fascination with them. Did she perhaps subconsciously understand how special they were? Is that why she took him there that day? Is it even possible that the child in her understood the secret of the birds? He didn't know. But he did know that she was captivated with their unerring ability to come back to her. Unaware of their instinctive ability, she claimed their love for her was the reason why they returned. How charming!

Learn a lesson or two from the magical birds, Aaron had said. Sam pictured them flying way up in the blue of the sky, circling a few times, as if setting course and direction. When they finally took off there was no stopping them. He remembered her watching them through binoculars, her excitement, as their circles grew wider. She knew the exact moment the birds selected their direction and began heading home to be with her! Sam realized suddenly that he could think of Karla without being miserable. Now he knew why. He had taken self-pity out of the equation; he was learning how to forgive himself.

He took a deep breath and said out loud. "Focus and clarity, I know it now. The birds possess it instinctively but we have to learn it intellectually. And that is why," he responded to Aaron's original question, "many people suffer as they do. They have no direction; they just drift endlessly on the wide-open ocean. They are like ships without rudders, all of them. Unlike the birds, that single-mindedly fly straight home."

"Well said." Aaron increased his pace. "The cross they bear is the weight of their unfulfilled, empty dreams. Because they never really pursued anything during their lifetime, they arrive at the doorstep of old age frustrated and unhappy, blaming everything for their discontent.

"One imagines that what is empty should be weightless, but an empty dream is a great drag. It tracks your trail and robs you of your sleep. The weight of an unfulfilled dream is determined by the measure of guilt you carry. Unfulfilled dreams result from wasted opportunities, mostly strangled by fear of failure. But the greatest indulgences are laziness and lack of interest.

"If, in old age you are angry and frustrated, lacking peace of mind, you might blame others but there is one fellow you cannot fool—guilt. Guilt shows up despite your assertion of innocence. It knows, and so do you. Unless you learn the art of self-forgiveness and change direction, nobody comes to relieve the weight of guilt. It follows you into the grave. There is no mercy for squandered talents, because only you can grant that pardon."

"What if you have neither talent nor opportunity? What if you were born without the capacity for understanding?" Sam asked.

Aaron halted briefly and half turned, glancing over his shoulder at Sam. "Those with lesser ability do not feel guilt, Sam, for they cannot. Guilt is always equal to your consciousness and therefore equal to your understanding. If the weight is heavy, the reckoning is with you."

"Unfulfilled dreams are the cross we carry." Sam was thinking out loud. "You're saying that the world is filled with frustrated, unhappy people because they lack inner direction. And if you lack inner direction, you're not really living; you are merely breathing."

Aaron smiled but didn't reply. They walked in silence for a while. Then a thought struck Sam. "Karla's magical birds . . ." He considered it carefully, trying to grasp the implication fully. "Aaron, if the birds are gifted with the instinct to determine direction and fly home, and we possess similar abilities, then we are all fulfilling our dreams and goals right now!"

"What does that insight mean, Sam?"

Sam stopped; Aaron turned, waiting. As Sam slowly spoke the words he recognized the truth of them. "It means that goal achievement for us is as automatic as it is for the birds. The problem is not goal achievement; it is goal setting, the inner direction you spoke of." They faced each other in the cold mountain air. "A state of perpetual unhappiness, frustration, or similar dissatisfaction is an indication of where our attention is focused. If we are going nowhere it is because of our inner states, the lack of direction.

"Lack of performance and thought processes must go hand in hand; they are the manifestations of the inner course we have selected, either unconsciously or by design. We are always moving in the direction of our dominant thoughts."

"Bravo." Aaron said softly. "I think you are gaining remarkable insight into your own life. But if it is that simple, why are there so many unhappy people with meaningless lives? If it is a matter of merely setting the course, why don't they do it?"

Sam grimaced in reply. "We are not taught to do it, not by our parents, and not in schools. We are not taught about the wonders and intricacies of how the mind functions. And," he added dramatically, "if we are told about the importance of inner direction and goal setting, it is so boring that few are interested."

"You never learn that boring leads to beautiful," Aaron replied. "You never learn that the ability to steer and control your life through clarity and focus is what puts your feet on the road to self-mastery." His face grew grave. "But if you don't learn this, then others govern your life. There are many millions who are governed by others, some because they have not yet progressed to a level of reasonable self-mastery, but just as many because they have relinquished that right through lack of interest."

Sam nodded. "This principle, if it is learned at all, is only introduced when the personality is already formed and the habits ingrained." He looked at Aaron. "Is this one of the Rules of the Game?"

Aaron resumed his stride. "It is the result of either not playing the game well or not knowing the rules. When you begin to understand the wonders of your own mind, inner direction becomes natural and automatic. When you gain insight into the mechanics of your most creative tool, life becomes the adventurous learning experience it was intended to be. You have to become enthralled with the possibilities of what the mind can accomplish so that you may understand your own creative ability."

Sam walked in silence behind him for a while, an indescribable joy slowly spreading through him. He knew he was on the brink of making some significant breakthroughs in his understanding, delving into aspects that in the past had caused his victimhood.

Mind waits for the input from us. It is as though it asks: what is it that you want? If we remain silent because we don't know the answer or if we are confused and frustrated, the mind can only do one thing, duplicate what it sees internally, which is nothing.

Sam gave a little laugh. "I see it, Aaron! Creation follows the Rules of the Game to the last iota. We cannot have externally what we cannot see internally in the mind's eye. Our true mission is to know ourselves, and in the quest of discovering our real nature, we find our creative ability. We discover thus that for each of us, our life is our own responsibility. And we create it, moment to moment.

"This is the inner direction you speak of. It is what Karla's magical birds automatically know, but we have to determine. The birds can only fly home but we can go anywhere we choose, if only we knew how to set the course!"

He heard Aaron chuckling. "I like that, Sam. You said it well. Now you know why mind is either your greatest ally or your most lethal foe. Consciously you have to decide what you want; for that you need clarity and focus. The more clarity and focus you have, the more detail the picture contains that imprints on the subconscious mind. The subconscious mind does not make decisions or choices; it takes everything you give it as fact. That is why its power is so magnificent, why it is the sleeping giant. It wakes up and transforms into a genie when you hand it the power of your own concentration. For then it can create wonders!

"If you emphasize some ideas through repetition, it begins to attract similar thoughts, events, and circumstances into your life that vibrate in harmony with your dominant thoughts. The circumstances of your life are always the result of what you've been thinking. The question is not what do I want? The question becomes what can I imagine?"

Aaron didn't break his stride. "But there is a tragedy hidden in that statement also, Sam. You know what it is, don't you?"

Sam followed his own line of thought. "With imagination we cross the barriers of reality and possibility. If we can imagine it and believe it, it can be ours. We become masters of our own destinies by learning how to create and understanding the Rules of the Game.

"The tragedy you speak of is a child who unlearns his ability to dream and visualize, cautioned by parents disillusioned by their own unfulfilled dreams not to expect too much from life. To borrow a phrase from you, they are benched early in life, denied a chance to learn the Rules of the Game by the example set by their caretakers.

"Instead of experiencing life as an opportunity, they see it as a life sentence of struggle. It is a lonely, bitter struggle. When imagination is curbed and dreams discouraged, when you are taught to be 'realistic' it is hard to imagine an alternative. And you'll never get to know your real self. Those on the bench rarely look within to understand their dilemmas. The habit of blaming others is already ingrained and seals their fate. They were never told as children to fill up on their dreams and thus old age finds them bitter, twisted, and disillusioned."

Sam saw the lights of the restaurant faintly in the distance. The fog had lifted considerably, and the outline of the buildings was much clearer. He thought it fitting that the fog was thinning on the mountain, and soon enough, the day would break fully.

For a fleeting moment he felt panic. Aaron would leave and he'd be on his own again. He thought about what the future might hold, and the uncertainty returned. Did he have enough time to turn his life around? How exactly would he accomplish that? What if Karla never changed her mind, or if she became sicker? He felt the knot in his stomach, weakening him in thought and stiffening his body. He felt very scared.

"Sam," Aaron stopped and looked up at the cloud ceiling lifting above them. "How does what you are doing right now serve you?"

"I'm not sure what you mean, Aaron," his voice was as uncertain as his heart felt. "I am still scared. I can't help that."

Aaron turned his gaze on him. "Tell me Sam, can you change anything that happened yesterday or the day before? Anything at all? The visit to the hospital, the meeting in the boardroom?"

"No."

"What is done is done?"

"I think so, yes."

"It is not good enough to just think so, Sam. I want you to tell me if there is any way in which you can change events that have already occurred."

"No," this time said with more conviction.

"Good. Now, I know that you can project yourself through imagination into future times, tomorrow, next week, five years from now, but can you live the actual moment before it arrives?"

"No."

"Why not, Sam?"

Sam stretched his thoughts to reach where Aaron was leading.

Of course!

He smiled sheepishly. "This moment is all I have. This very moment, now."

Aaron waited.

"And since I can't change the past, or live a future moment before it arrives," he spoke slowly, "it follows that whenever my mind dwells in the past, or attempts to inhabit the future, I am effectively powerless." Sam's voice had a pensive quality. "And that means that agonizing over water under the bridge or tomorrow's challenges is a waste of energy. It accomplishes nothing except to compound the problem.

"But our race does this from habit, Aaron! We brood over our problems, our losses, our dilemmas, our heartaches, the list is endless. We learn this reaction from our parents or other role models. And we don't question it. On the contrary, it goes quietly under the radar as normal human behavior. Worry is accepted behavior because everyone does it, and it is associated with being responsible. It is intended to demonstrate you care!"

"I see. So, it is no good worrying about the past, but what of the future, Sam? Surely you must plan for the future? What happens to your goals, if you don't plan?"

Sam spoke without hesitation, "To live in the present moment does not mean that you abandon your life. To live in the moment means you have to be a more conscious and aware human being. You must be conscious enough to know when your mind is dwelling needlessly in the past or irrationally fearing the future. One who plans for the future has a different attitude than one who fears it. When you fear the future, you are expecting a negative outcome.

"At a very deep level you don't believe that you deserve the good and therefore cannot, and don't expect it. You helped me to discover these two major Rules of the Game. Belief creates the possibility, and if belief is firm, then expecting the good is a natural, given result. The universe delivers, not by chance but because of clear focus. And it never doubts your intention because it follows your dominant thoughts. It registers your energy fingerprint and, reading your ID accurately, it realizes your dream masterfully, through design."

"And right now we are still on the mountain." Aaron spoke deliberately. "What you have is this moment. You already know all your power is right here, now. No amount of fretting or worrying about anything, including Karla, will influence the outcome in your favor. It will, however, shape your emotions and cloud your judgment. If you deal responsibly with your life, on a moment-to-moment basis, your mind will be clear, and you'll be able to face any challenge ahead of you. It will no longer be weighed down by your imagined fears.

"Sam, if you can train your mind to look at a challenge and rename it opportunity, a magnificent paradigm shift occurs. With the paradigm shift comes enormous possibilities for problem solving. Your focus is redirected from brooding over the problem to finding solutions. And that is the essence of solving all problems. But you need an aware mind to do this, don't you Sam? Worriers sit on the bench because their attention is in the wrong place."

Sam stood quite still, considering the implications of their discussion. When they had first met, Aaron did all the talking and he listened. He noticed that from the time of their second visit to the cliff, their roles seemed to become equal: he, Sam, did as much talking as Aaron.

Aaron was right, if he learned to focus his attention in the present moment he could handle anything. Even if the outcome was less than perfect, at least he would not be burdened by the additional negative buildup he usually indulged in. "I lost track of time," he said looking around them at the light slowly seeping in everywhere.

"Relax, Sam. There is enough time," Aaron replied, as they started walking toward the deserted buildings. "Living your life in the present moment is a sign of an adult, conscious human being."

"Can a child do this, Aaron?"

"Children do it naturally. It is their role models who unconsciously teach them their negative behavior responses, and only because they don't know any better. Sam, it does not matter if you live to see twenty or ninety; that is merely growing older, and growing older is mandatory. What matters is that you also grow up in this time. Growing up is optional, for you may choose not to."

Sam thought of his schooldays and the behavior of many of his teammates' parents when, as a child, he had played soccer. Their angry, contorted faces when they disagreed with a game official; the shouted obscenities from the sideline; and the humiliation on his teammates' faces. If these parents had been aware, they would have seen that they were expecting their children to settle the scores of their own unfulfilled dreams, offloading the guilt of their failures on their innocent offspring.

"You are thinking of one who has forgotten where he is and vexingly finds himself back in his own childhood. Such a man does not comprehend that the joy and the lesson are both in the moment, and offer a great opportunity for introspection.

"If the parent demands restitution from the sideline, the child is denied the lesson, no matter what the offense is. Such a child is not taught to solve a problem, but to force his own way. His parent's behavior does not demonstrate that unfairness is an attribute of a world with so many pluralistic perceptions. Instead, the parent's behavior rejects tolerance and truth on the grounds of who he is. Ironically, this is something he does not even know himself!

"The greatest failure in raising children has not been lack of love or good intentions. Most parents mean well. It is the blindness to see that children follow example. They don't listen to words. They do what you do, not what you say.

"They have their individual traits and talents, but they watch your behavior and then shape these after you. If you forget yourself, then so will they."

"The sins of the fathers ..." Sam hesitated.

"Are handed down from one generation to the next, on all levels, through the living example of the parents, or other role models," Aaron finished.

"But what sin is this? I know my mind made the connection but I can't quite articulate it."

"If transgressions have degrees, then the supreme sin is committed against the Self: failure to know thyself. Without adequate self-knowledge—a focused probe to understand your behavior and your responses—you unconsciously select the path of your role models. You do as they did; you defend, love, and hate the same things. Despite the amazing technological revolution, in thousands of years, society itself has not taken one step forward. It cannot, because so few individuals do; the forward movement of society depends on the progress of individuals.

"You realized earlier tonight how Karla and you both imitated your parents' behavior, even though you thought you wanted something different.

"Your example of the sports field is a good one because children watch their parents and then imitate them. Anyone serious about self-improvement and growth knows another can't harm him without his permission. Certainly he notices infractions also, but he makes an effort to restrain himself; he knows his child learns from him.

"Every time he catches himself in the moment and overcomes the impulse to lose control, his perspective improves. He sees the activity for what it is—a game of sports—not a measure of his personal value.

"Displaying anger or alleging that another has slighted you—either through deed or innuendo—displays lack of self-knowledge and demonstrates where the consciousness is. Thus, if through uncontrolled, angry outbursts, or name-calling, you teach your child the opposite of self-control, the pattern is set and ingrained each time you repeat it.

"Obviously, the claim that you descend from a family of hotheads, bad-tempered folks, and that it runs in the family is nothing but a lame excuse to be rude. It does not run in the genes, it is absent from the consciousness and awareness, stemming from lack of self-knowledge. An unaware parent sets the example and it is passed on from generation to generation. But it is curable. An open mind and a brave heart is where it starts."

"Why a brave heart?"

"Why, you need to be brave, because if you look in the mirror, you might not like what you see. And if you try to break away from the mainstream, others will come after you with a vengeance.

"But there is no other way. You learn from self-observation, watching your responses, moment to moment, not from dwelling in the past or living in the future. When you practice self-observation, you teach your child that authentic growth is internal."

They were back at the restaurant, in the same place where they had begun their conversation hours earlier. Sam was aware of how tired he was. He had gone through this entire night, treading the paths on the mountain in Aaron's company, and had never thought of sleep. The experience held a dreamlike quality. He was sure, though, that he did not want to wake.

"So much has happened, Aaron. How can I possibly hope to recall all of it?"

"Write the book," Aaron said.

Sam looked at him incredulously. "You said this before." Aaron didn't reply.

Sam sat in one of the outdoor chairs. Aaron remained standing. "There is one more thing that we have to discuss. Tonight we discussed the secrets of creation. But there is also a secret to life, the art of living, if you will. You cannot do without it. Everyone interested in self-development and growth must know it. And that secret is balance. Without balance, life slowly begins to self-destruct."

▲ ▲ ▲

Balance

"*B*alance is the key to spiritual growth and to coping with the demands of your life." Aaron's voice was a soft murmur. "Look around you, all of nature speaks of balance. It is evident in the natural rhythm of day and night, in the ebb and flow of the oceans, the waxing and waning of the moon, and the path that earth follows around the sun.

"If you could see far enough into the night sky to observe the stars and the planets, you would understand balance. The heavenly bodies hold each other perfectly in place. Balance is the natural state of the universe." He smiled, "There is a time for everything. Respect for this principle does wonders for establishing balance."

Sam looked around him. The mountain sat still and quiet, waiting for the day to unfold. He glanced over at Aaron, sitting down with his legs stretched out in front of him. He looked relaxed and rested. Sam thought about the possibilities that lay ahead and he felt the excitement stir in him. He said, "There is one more thing about balance you wanted to mention."

Aaron looked up, smiling openly. "You are reading my mind, Sam?"

Sometime in the course of the night, Sam realized, the lessons had evolved into a dialogue between equals.

"You are thinking of wisdom."

"Yes." Sam said. "You must do quite a bit of living before you learn balance, but somewhere along the way, I assume, wisdom and perception also become your companions. Wisdom is not cleverness," he emphasized. "Wisdom never comes to a person who does not know himself. Wisdom is learned at every step on the way as we seek to understand ourselves. Every time we work on developing ourselves, we move toward balance. And we lose interest in judging others, for judging others is our feeble attempt to distract attention away from our own shortcomings. We have our own lives to live, and we must trust that others, in their own time, will touch the same ideal." As Sam spoke, he stretched his arms and rubbed the back of his neck. He began to yawn.

"Yes, Sam, you have your life to live. As all rivers inevitably flow to the ocean, when the time is right, humans connect to their Source. It is inevitable."

"It is inevitable," Sam echoed, and closing his eyes for a moment he felt the pleasant feeling of drifting away. Then he opened them with a start. "Did I fall asleep?"

"You are very tired." Aaron pointed to a spot behind Sam. "See that grassy patch over there? Why not rest for a while? If you close your eyes, we can still talk. The first cable car won't be coming up the mountain until eight."

Sam nodded, aware of how exhausted he was. He got up and walked over to the grass where he stretched out on the soft, slightly damp surface. Then he closed his eyes, put an arm up to block out the faint light and relaxed into the soothing sound of Aaron's voice.

In the chair where he sat, Aaron also closed his eyes. "The difficulty is in maintaining balance. When you discover something that you find exciting, you can spoil your discovery with hyperactivity and exaggeration. When you do not strive for balance, you overemphasize what you have found, and you create distance between you and others, especially those whom you intend to help, or want to convince.

"It is so with new faith. Some become street-corner preachers; others change this faith for that one, and in believing they found the only one, they crusade to save the world causing an intelligent person to feel contempt. Others don't hear your message, they only see the uncompromising glint in your eye and in the absence of balance, you lose them.

"It is so in the world of commerce, where the only priority is profit. When the scales are not balanced between giving and taking, the poor cannot see any virtue in your fortune and may grow to hate you. Soon they will plot to take your fortune from you, and you'll pay a high price for your safety and your worldly goods.

"Growth depends on balance, and without balance, man becomes one-dimensional and loses touch with his world. He constantly falls in the direction he leans hardest, that of his obsession. You were meant to live in this world, if that were not so, you wouldn't be here."

Sam's entire body was relaxed. He heard Aaron's voice, soft and deep in the background, words and meaning woven beautifully into a fabric of understanding; a certain knowing his subconscious mind accepted, recognized as familiar. For a moment he wondered how he knew, it was as if an invisible hand had parted the curtain. He brought his attention back to the moment.

"You said earlier that our world naturally maintains its balance. But looking at the world, I find that hard to believe. Here in Africa, and elsewhere, famine claims the lives of tens of thousands every year. But on the other side of the world, obesity fills the purses of the multi-billion dollar diet industry, and other related industries—all geared to saving us from willful self-destruction. We send spacecraft to the

Moon and Mars and spend billions of dollars on wars, while millions live here, homeless, illiterate, starving, and suffering. If our lives depend on the health of our planet, why do we pollute the air, kill the forests, deplete the oceans, and poison our waters? Destruction and imbalance scream from every corner of the world. We are suffocating the very source of our existence. We continue to fail ourselves. Our limited perspective worships the false gods of arrogance, hate, anger, power, and money. We sacrifice balance in the name of progress."

"Humankind's progress depends on the progress of each individual," Aaron interjected softly. "We have already established this. But you speak of those who govern, who take charge, politically, economically, and religiously. They always claim what they do is for the greater good of the people, but that is rarely true. They act for the greater benefit of themselves, to guarantee their power. Most people are not yet ready to govern themselves, and that is why there is a system in place electing officials to do it for them. The reason for the shocking corruption in the higher echelons is clear—the consciousness of the governors is equal to the people. The Law of Attraction dictates that."

"What would a society where the people can govern themselves look like?" Sam asked. A long silence followed. Sam thought that Aaron had dozed off. He didn't look or make a move; he just allowed the question to hang in the air.

When Aaron finally spoke, his voice seemed to come from far away. "In a self-governing society, people would love and honor themselves because, through devotion to honest self-assessment, they would truly know themselves. Holy Scripture tells us to love God as you would love yourself. In a self-governing society, that directive is known and practiced.

"People would know God because they have traveled the path that leads within. No one can love or honor God without coming along this way. The narrow, difficult path is to get to know you. People live oblivious to their true natures. They waste their time in elaborate ego building practices, consciously seeking out ways to elevate themselves in their own eyes and the eyes of others.

"They may pretend humility, but they judge with a fierceness that is equaled only by the anger that consumes them for those who don't think like them, or believe like them. They are incapable of honest introspection and thus, cannot get to know who they really are.

"A society capable of self-government lives according to the code of honor that people in your world only preach about. In your world, hypocrites apply this code to judge others, but rarely practice what they preach."

"You cannot honor and love God without honoring and loving yourself," Sam continued. "You cannot reach the Source without knowing yourself first, and that cannot happen if you don't see yourself as you are."

Aaron's face softened with a smile but he kept his eyes closed as he finished Sam's thought. "An individual who takes responsibility for himself doesn't need external laws to restrain him. Internal laws govern him. He understands the Rules of the Game; he knows he creates his own reality. He knows that he is the lawmaker of his own life, and he decides what is possible. He respects and honors those around him, for like him, they are on a journey also. And he lets them be—trusting they'll find their way. When another finds the way more readily, he applauds that person, and shares his or her joy. He never competes for spiritual supremacy, for he understands the journey is not a competition. There is room for everyone. Those who think they are competing, feel themselves to be unworthy and dwell in spiritual darkness.

"Instead, he has compassion for himself as he makes mistakes and learns, and regards others with the same kindness, for he knows that he must first gain insight into his own life; only then can he hope to understand others. Ironically, in your world, people constantly struggle in their attempts to reverse this rule, the inside-out approach.

"Conscious, aware humans know that what they do for or against themselves benefits or harms every other person, and thus they choose wisely. A person such as this can live under any law. He neither requires nor disregards the law. A balanced, aware man feels no sense of rebellion. He understands the rhythm and flow of the universe and he knows the Law of Energy which creates everything. He knows that a rebel's attention is on what is wrong, but he chooses to give his attention to what is right."

"Stress slips in the backdoor," Sam said, barely audible, "when balance leaves."

He wasn't sure if he were dreaming the conversation. He floated in a warm, comfortable space, his muscles and mind, relaxed. He felt the rhythmic beating of his heart under the hand covering his chest. "It is hard for us though, Aaron," he murmured. The words came out slowly like one surrendering to sleep, "We learn from the moment we are born that life's a rat race. We learn to chase the same phantoms, to run heedlessly at the same crazy pace as our role models teach us. If life disillusioned our parents early, we adopt caution and fear as a way of life and learn to expect the negative, constantly bracing against the onslaught of disappointments.

"If they lack balance, then we do the same. If we do not awaken, we continue to live like sheeple. We follow the followers, always searching for someone to blame."

Sam's chest rose and fell evenly as he began to sleep. Someone was speaking. Aaron—or maybe him. He let the words fill every atom of his being. "Waking is hard because you have to fight the conditioning and negative responses people have adopted since the beginning of time. When you blindly follow the example of others, you begin to value what they value.

"It takes a huge conversion of energy to dislodge from your established momentum. Perhaps you need to experience a total breakdown to cause you to question if what you have is what you really want. If the answer is no, it takes a brave man to look in the mirror and admit he doesn't like what he sees. And you'll need more courage to admit that what you thought you valued perhaps no longer serves you.

"People talk about their values, but we value only that which we devote time to. Without that focus, what we claim to value is a conversation topic, nothing more. Many say they value balance, but their harried, frustrated lives contradict the claim. Balance is difficult to achieve. It asks for an open mind, it needs moderation and it depends on maturity. Only then does balance come.

"Balance smoothes the brow of worry and restores the joy of living. It reveals the truth that life is as you make it. It allows you the freedom to give weight to one thing, and remove the heaviness of another. Balance is living life on your terms, and still being emotionally healthy. Then you'll know joy and happiness, because you chose it, and you caused it.

"Balance is respecting the physical body but knowing that it is merely the shell for the spiritual, the immortal. The physical body is an expression of the sum total of consciousness the individual holds. The physical represents what was chosen at incarnation to provide a vehicle for its learning. In its eternal wisdom, the soul weaves an intricate fabric of all your past experience, your knowledge, your insight, your growth, and your challenges and presents it to you as opportunity in the body you now have, in the circumstances in which you are born. Balance teaches you to honor the body as the house in which your spirit lives. It reveals that being in this world but not of this world is much more than an empty religious value.

"Balance assumes a fundamental understanding of the three expressions of man. A fully awake man acknowledges he expresses his animal needs through the physical, his mental needs through reason, and he constantly discovers the divine through daily inspiration. The degree to which you are able to express yourself in all three depends entirely on your consciousness. And your consciousness is measured by the balance of which you are capable.

"In the physical body with its limitations, aware man discovers the wonders of the mind, and connects mind and body as components of the same being. In studying the mind he discovers the finer expression of the same being no longer as an invisible dream existing in description only, but discerns it as an ethereal reality, very close and within reach.

"He finds his own immortality and gains insight into spirit; his true essence, and then his inspirational side comes alive, and begins to blossom. He discards self-righteousness and petty thinking. Finally, he is ready for the real adventures of the universe which are not of this world, neither are they in this world, but the path leading there is from this world."

Sam woke at the sound of a horn. A ship on the surface of the ocean far below was announcing its intention to enter the harbor. He opened his eyes. The fog had completely dissipated; he was bathed in cloudless sunlight. It was very quiet.

He sat up and looked around him. "Aaron?" He was completely alone.

Sam stood slowly and turned around, looking in all directions. There was nobody. He locked his fingers behind his head, squeezed his eyes shut, and breathed deeply. He opened his eyes slowly. He looked at the chair where Aaron had been sitting a few hours before; it was empty, facing away from the other chairs.

Sam felt bewildered.

Had he been hallucinating? Had he dreamed away the whole night?

He started walking toward the closest lookout point. When he reached the wall, he carefully stepped up close, and then looked over the edge. The mountainside was alive with activity. To the left, far below the cliff at the foot of the mountain, a group of hikers snaked their way up. It was early for them to be out, but then it would take them a while to reach the summit.

His eye caught the graceful movement of two small indigenous mountain buck making their way over the rough terrain of the mountain. Sam watched them find invisible footholds to carry them forward; they appeared to have wings. He smelled the delicate fragrances of the flowers carried on the early morning breeze. An indescribable happiness filled his heart. *Thank you, Aaron.*

He sat down with his back against the wall and felt the welcome sunshine on his face. He stretched his legs in front of him and closed his eyes to await the arrival of the first cable car.

How could he tell others of this night? Who would believe him? He knew it didn't matter what others believed. It mattered what he believed. Write a book, Aaron had said. *I will do that, if only to remember what I have learned this past night. What shall I name it?*

"The Rules of the Game."

"Aaron?" Sam opened his eyes swiftly. *Did I fall asleep again?* He looked around, not really expecting to find anyone. He was still completely alone. He heard the grinding cables, and saw, far below, the first car moving on its way up. He heard the voices shrieking in excitement as the car twirled and revolved slowly, displaying the magnificence of the mountain in its summer colors.

Sam waited patiently; he felt no hurry to get off the mountain. His fear had left him. His fear had become anticipation of a new beginning. *I'll bring Karla here. She will understand.*

Sam was the only passenger returning on the first run down the mountain. He sat back, relaxed, as the car swung out of the berth and heaved itself over the cliff to start its slow, circular dance down the cables. His stomach felt strange but he concentrated on the vista he saw from the window.

What a magnificent place! What an unusual experience. Karla.

▲   ▲   ▲

The Palette with Which I Paint

Sam pulled into the visitors' parking lot. Visiting hours were not until the afternoon, but he decided not to worry about that as he made his way to the front entrance.

The familiar smell of stale coffee and disinfectant permeated the hallway. Sam shuddered as he walked purposefully down the wide, polished corridor leading to the psychiatric wing.

She doesn't belong here. He walked faster.

How will I approach her? How will I explain?

His mind refused to consider the rejection of a few days ago. "That was then. This is now," he was surprised to hear himself say the words out loud.

I am not looking back again. His determination increased.

Then he was in front of her door, and for a moment his courage deserted him. The door was slightly open as if someone had forgotten to close it properly. Sam stood outside, head down and palm on the door, hesitating. He was afraid but relieved to admit it. *I cannot make her decisions for her.*

The last time he was here he had left empty-handed. She would not see him. He squeezed his eyes shut briefly. That was two days ago, and nothing had changed for her.

He couldn't consider the possibility of not seeing her, and pushed against the door. It swung open soundlessly. Karla . . .

She was sitting upright in the bed, looking directly at him. The shock of seeing each other showed instantly on both their faces. She slowly caught her breath, and her face lost all expression. Sam stood paralyzed. He had imagined she would be asleep, that he would have time to be close to her, time to find the right words. But there was no time, they were face-to-face and there was no turning back. His heart sank as she sat motionless, looking at him. He saw shock mixed with surprise, as if she were trying to understand something. He was unable to speak, unable to move.

Her eyes slowly filled with tears that did not spill, a distinct way of hers to prevent emotion sweeping her away—a peculiarity that had intrigued him since their childhood. Her face held the power to break his heart. Sam stood staring, unsure how to reach out to her or how to undo his coming here.

Incredibly, Karla moved first. She held her hand out to him; the tears finally spilled over and streaked down her pale cheeks. "Oh God. Sam . . .!"

He found himself beside her bed, bending over her, speechless and trembling. She reached up and cupped his face in her hands. "I'm so glad you came back," she whispered. Sam closed his eyes and felt her warm breath against his cheek as she spoke into his ear. *It wasn't over!*

"I thought you'd be sleeping. I'm so sorry. I didn't mean to alarm you." He wasn't sure if he had said the words aloud, for she continued talking softly against his face as if she hadn't heard.

"I woke just after five this morning; I didn't know what woke me. But I knew I wasn't alone, and then I saw you sitting in the chair over there." She turned her head almost imperceptibly to indicate the chair at the foot of the bed.

Sam opened his eyes, looking into hers. A shiver ran through his body and he put his cheek against hers. "Karla, my darling, that's not possible . . ." He muffled the last word as he slid his arms around her warm body, burying his face in the softness of her neck, smelling her hair. His mind raced as she kept whispering, her mouth delicately against his ear, her hands tangled in his hair.

"How did you get in at that hour, Sam?" she asked with a little unstable sob.

"Karla, what?" Her words confused him but he let her speak, not understanding. He wondered if it was the drugs they were giving her, he didn't know, but he far preferred this incoherent woman clinging to him than nothing at all. He would have her any way.

"I was so glad to see you but I didn't know if I was dreaming. I thought I had lost my mind, Sam. And I was so scared you would disappear again. I was afraid I would drive you away, so I didn't speak to you. It was just so comforting to see you sitting there. I'm so sorry; I must have fallen asleep again. Sam, please don't leave!" She cried softly, her face hidden in his hair, her body trembling, telling of the loss she felt for the baby and for what they once had.

He tightened his grip around her waist. "Karla . . ." Sam struggled to find his voice; he struggled with the onslaught of the different emotions and realizations simultaneously rushing into his awareness. He felt Karla's body in his arms and his physical self responded instantly, pulling her hard up against him, molding her into his frame. Terror, pity, and wonder filled his heart.

His mind disjointedly considered the possibility of her words. He didn't even know if he could reach a reasonable conclusion. And then there was a piece of him that stood apart in neutral observation. Sam saw the crooked smile, the quiet nod of the head. "Aaron . . . Karla, my darling, we have to talk." He released her gently, and ran his hands through her long, thick hair, comforting her and being comforted. *Where do I start?*

He was afraid to let go of her, afraid that she would disappear if he took his hands off her. With his arms about her, he took hold of the long hair at her back and wound two thick locks around the fingers of both hands; then he closed his fists and pulled gently on her hair. She looked up at him.

Sam held her gaze. "This has been a very unusual night, Karla," he said slowly, "And I know that you will find this difficult to believe," he said, his voice deep and soft, "but I spent it on top of Table Mountain where I had the most extraordinary meeting."

She looked at him while he held her hair, her eyes clearing. "You're terrified of heights, my Sam," she said softly, mystified by his unusual revelation about the mountain.

He stared back at her. Then he lifted her out of the bed and pulled her close to him again, he gently kissed her crown, and over her head he looked at the chair she had spoken of. *What was she talking about?* He didn't know. He closed his eyes and held her in his embrace.

The sound of a hospital trolley reverberated noisily down the corridor. Karla leaned away from him, then reached up on her toes and linked her hands around his neck, tangling her fingers in his hair, accidentally pulling it. Sam winced, and drew his head away to relieve the pressure. "I think it is time to cut my hair." He smiled down at her.

"Oh no!" She feigned horror. "I have always loved your ponytail. It does not suit a lot of men but it sits well on you. Your hair is so strong and thick, and besides," she reached up to lay an open palm on the side of his head, "you never grow it past your shoulders." He nodded in compliance, while she continued. "When we were children, all the girls envied your hair. I fell in love with you the way you are. Please?"

Sam's heart swelled with love. She was still the mesmerizing girl of twelve asking to be picked up so she could show off her magical birds. His thoughts returned to the mountain and the mystery of his visitor. "Aaron . . ." This time he said it louder.

Karla looked at him curiously. "That's the second time," she whispered.

He still did not know what or how to tell her. "What is?" he asked, picking her up and setting her gently down on the bed.

"You know, Sam, Aaron is your first name," she said tentatively, "and you've used it twice now. Why?" She smiled at him. "I wonder why your parents did not call you by that name. It suits you so well."

Sam leaned forward and touched his lips to her forehead. "Oh God, Karla this is so hard to explain. I'm not even sure I know how to put it into words." He closed his eyes. Then he felt her hands go around his face.

"Sam . . ." The noise in the hallway came closer and he tensed, expecting an orderly or nurse to appear in the doorway any minute. "Don't mind them," she said, still cupping his face with her hands. "What is it, Sam? What is so hard to explain?"

"Karla," Sam could hear his own heart beat. "I did go to the mountain last night. I went there to lose myself permanently." He swallowed hard. "Instead, incredibly, I found myself," he finished softly.

Karla sat very still, watching him, her hands still about his face. "How did you get down the mountain in the dark?" she asked softly, tenderly tracing a finger from his temple to the corner of his mouth.

Sam took the hand in front of his mouth and kissed the tips of her fingers, and then wrapped the small hand in his own. "That is part of what we both still have to figure out," he said earnestly. "Karla, I only came down the mountain this morning."

She stared at him, her eyes incredulous, weighing his statement carefully. "Sam?" she whispered softly, searching his face. He held her gaze, waiting. Then she smiled tenderly and put her head lightly against his shoulder. She responded with conviction. "No, my darling, I know when you're near me. It is not possible to fool me, not with you." She looked up and found his eyes. "I claimed you years ago at the birdcage, remember? I'll know you always, and I know you were here, Sam."

His eyes were filled with love. "I believe you." It was an effortless truth. He sat down on the bed beside her, pulling her into his arms. "You don't belong here, Karla," he said firmly, "but we'll deal with that later." He tightened his embrace as he spoke with his mouth in her hair. "First, I'm going to tell you about the mountain and the terrible abyss." He stroked her hair softly. "And then I want to tell you of the man that died on the mountain." He put a hand under her chin and turned her face toward him. She closed her eyes and for a moment he just looked at the lovely, still face in his hands. "Then I'll tell you of the man who was born." Sam dropped a soft kiss on each eye. "This way, you'll understand about the man I met."

For a long time it was quiet in the room, and he wondered if she had fallen asleep. Sam heard her breathing rhythmically against his chest, but then she looked up at him and whispered, "His name was Aaron?"

Her words were a statement of a subconscious knowing that instantly overwhelmed him and he couldn't respond. He tightened his arms about her and he held her close to his heart.

They became aware of the other person at the same time. The woman standing on the other side of the bed was shaking a thermometer. She looked somewhat embarrassed. "I'm sorry. I don't mean to interrupt." She stared, visibly baffled, at Sam. "Sir, you must be very tired!" She glanced briefly at the watch pinned to her uniform, looked at the chair at the end of the bed, and then brought her gaze back to them. "Pardon me," she averted her glance. "I apologize. It's been a long night."

Sam stood aside as she put the thermometer in Karla's mouth, and then took her pulse. The nurse kept her eyes on the pinned watch.

It took some convincing and a fair deal of negotiation, but Sam fetched her from the hospital three days later, on a glorious summer's day.

"Where are we going?" she asked as he opened the car door for her. She had put her thick hair in a French braid.

Sam watched the sunlight reflect the sleekness of it. He smiled at her.

"Away from here." He looked at the hospital behind them, helping her into the car. "It's such a beautiful day, and it is quite a drive, but why don't we visit Cape Agullas?"

"The southernmost point of the continent. Is that symbolic of something, Sam?"

He looked at her before starting the car. "Perhaps. I don't know yet. There is symbolism in so many things. I am only now learning to recognize it and follow my inspiration as it reveals itself." He leaned over, brushing her cheek with his mouth. "Like missing the symbolism of your magical birds, years ago." He grinned, "But perhaps I can be forgiven, for my heart was bewitched that day."

She laughed and buried her face in his shoulder. "When you speak I can see, feel what is in your mind." Then she looked at him somberly. "Before, you would not communicate, you stopped talking to me."

Sam put two fingers on her lips, and shook his head. "That was then. Not anymore." He made up his mind. "Let's go. We have much to talk about. I want to tell you about the rules of game, so we can both play." He put the car in gear and backed out of the parking space. "How would you like to go for a walk on a beach, and put your feet in the same water that also touches the icy shores of the South Pole?"

▲ ▲ ▲

Karla sat behind him on the sand, resting her cheek against his back. The sun wrapped them warmly together. "What a magnificent experience," she said softly, her voice filled with wonder. "You must write the book, Sam." She dug her fingers into the warm sand, touching coolness beneath the surface.

Sam remained motionless and didn't respond immediately. She could faintly hear his heart beating; and there was something just so wonderfully intimate about that. He soaked up the heat behind his closed eyelids, basking in the depth of his happiness, the genuine love he felt for her, a love that seemed to include everything, everyone.

"Yes, I know." He gathered her from behind him, placing her loosely in his lap, facing the ocean. He put his arms around her waist and pulled her closely into his body, resting his chin in the familiar hollow of her shoulder. "I want to do it for us more than anything else. If it helps other people, then that's wonderful. But I never want to forget . . ." he caught himself and changed his words purposely, "I always want to remember that extraordinary meeting with Aaron."

For a while they both listened to the crashing of the waves on the beach. Each time the water came rushing across the wet sand, the foam reached nearer to where they sat on the warm, sandy hill above the waterline. They didn't move.

"How will you be able to remember everything, Sam? It is not always easy to recall how a conversation unfolded." He marveled at how easily she accepted his account of that night, how unconditionally she trusted him.

"This is different. On the mountain, Aaron assured me I would remember. He never allowed me to become sidetracked by trivialities; he thought of that as a minor detail." Sam moved into deep reverie. "Nor did he allow me to get away with any of my avoidance tactics."

"What do you mean?" she whispered, turning her head sideways to catch his answer over the sound of the ocean. Sam took a deep breath and dropped a light kiss on her hair. "You," he said simply, "and little Phoebe." He heard her draw her breath in, felt her tighten.

"No, Karla," he said, his mouth close to her ear. "Don't do that. Please don't do that. There is no need for us to explain or justify anything to each other anymore." He spoke softly but he knew she heard every word, "We both made mistakes, but we made them out of ignorance. Neither of us knew any better. And little Phoebe didn't drive us apart, my darling. She brought us together."

She lay back against him, the memory of the tiny body vividly in front of her. She couldn't stop the tears. Phoebe, so small, and so beyond help, gracefully accepting her fate. Sam felt her distress, but waited silently. Karla had to come to terms with the baby's death, not from his perspective, but from her own. She had to learn to lean away from her pain, not constantly fall into it. She had to search for the true meaning of Phoebe's presence in her life.

"He spoke to you about our baby?" She buried her face in his neck, silently pleading for support. He could barely hear her.

Sam pulled her away gently so he could see her face. "Aaron said that I would understand about Phoebe. He was right, and that is happening still. The understanding is an ongoing process." He looked away from her, his eyes on the restless ocean before them and spoke slowly, almost with reverence. "The fullness, the perfection of our baby's short life is unfolding in me, moment to moment. I now know that she gave her place up to you. As important as she was, she came after you. You are the one I couldn't be without. Her loss brought us back together by leading me up the mountain and to Aaron. You truly are my magical bird, Karla; my heart does not doubt that."

She lay still in his arms, holding on to every word.

"Somehow, with our conditioned, negative behavior patterns, our selfish needs, our terrible insecurities, and despite our love for each other, she was caught in the middle. All the self-absorption made it harder for us to remember the magnificence of what we had, what we found all those years ago when we were merely children."

She stirred at the memory, and he looked at her. "We were supposed to be sublimely happy; instead we deteriorated into a miserable couple, wanting and needing each other but incapable of getting in touch with ourselves, much less each other. What bound us was an innocent babe. And the undoing of that bond, painful as it is, set us free to find truth, to find each other again. Before she died, we were well on our way to repeating our parents' mistakes. We were going to teach Phoebe those mistakes, to be just like us."

"What a loss that would have been," Karla said quietly. Her eyes shone but she didn't cry. "Phoebe must be such a happy little soul, and wise beyond her years to reunite her parents in this way."

Sam smiled at Karla's insight. "When we're born we are handed a clean canvas," he said, "on which we can paint anything we choose; we can create to our hearts desire. But it is not that simple.

"The challenge of the human race is the conditioning introduced during the formative years when the child is helpless to influence decisions made on his behalf. He is without personal power and lacks life experience. He is forced to follow the examples before him. He literally takes the palette from his role models and begins to paint like them. If what he sees stimulates him to learn about his world and himself, he paints with the flair of a budding artist. His creativity grows, if Spirit is allowed to lead the way.

"But if what he sees is bleak and fearful, his paintings will mirror this paradigm of limitation. The canvas will depict his dangerous world where luck or fate determines his share of happiness, or success.

"The real tragedy is that many die in old age caught in the same consciousness they were born with. Not because they never had the chance to grow and expand, but because they preferred the safety of the city walls where the tribe pays homage to the group ego that rules them. It is very hard to escape from this conceited ego; its special skill is to discourage individuality and its slogan is 'safety in numbers.'

"From inside the walls it is difficult to see how cleverly ego contrives to seek self-importance, how it demands recognition and slyly coaxes the unaware. Few who live here can see how experienced ego is at exploiting humility to sway others to think like them, believe like them, and do their bidding. Those who do see it, start planning their escape the same day.

"In the endless physical and spiritual wars of our world, winning is coveted so you can boast of dominance and strength; paradoxically, both are driven by a terrible fear. The soldiers in military war march under the brutal orders of an invisible, but ruthless general, called Ego. It controls their leaders who send them off to the battlefields to die for their selfish causes. The price of ignorance in war is very high. If you kill another you have only two commodities to trade with, peace of mind and blood. Many lose both.

"Spiritually, the ruse is subtler but the battle is just as merciless. They quarrel over this religion or that one, my god or your god; they don't see the master puppeteer pulling the strings to make them dance. He too goes by the name of Ego.

"Ego blinds you; its brilliance is to hide You from you. It keeps you in a holding pattern of trivial, tribal disputes for supremacy, judgment, and conditional everything. It shackles and binds you to the very sins you pray so hard to be forgiven for. And Ego laughs hard, for it sits comfortably on this side of the abyss, jealously guarding the path to You, who waits undisturbed, patiently on the other side of your obsessions, your suffocating need to be right.

"Ego trains you through habit to toe the line, not to question and investigate anything that could cause its abdication. So it reminds you constantly of social acceptance, it points to the quagmire of your blind, dogmatic beliefs, your cherished conditioned responses and thoughts, and it whispers cruelly in you ear: You plan to pass this way, dearest?

"Breaking free of tribal thinking is the single most important thing any individual can accomplish. It is the first chink in the armor of the ego to go. You have to withstand subtle but enormously powerful social pressures. Innuendo that your interests are outside the boundaries of the accepted, or not quite respectable, has driven many to a life of mediocrity. They are timidly brought back inside the city walls, into the fold of the dull, sameness of the crowd where individuality is a marble tomb to which they pay homage in the town square."

"Sam, is this you talking?" she sat up and looked at him.

Sam stood and pulled her into his arms, murmuring over her head. "You've always fit so perfectly under my chin, Karla. This way you're not only in my heart but you're so close to it."

She smiled against his chest, feeling the warmth of his skin through his shirt and loving the familiarity of it. She thought of the experience on the mountain he had shared with her. "So you were angry when he called it a game?"

He nodded, recalling the dismay he had felt. "I didn't know who he was and I wasn't thinking straight, but mostly, I didn't want him to interfere with my dreadful plan."

She shuddered and pressed her face in his shoulder. "I'm so glad he stopped you, Sam."

He took her face in his hands and held it until she looked at him. Then he kissed her lips softly. "So am I," he whispered against her mouth. "See the lighthouse over there?" he looked up, over her head. "The view is breathtaking from there. Come, let's go." He put an arm around her shoulders and led her up the winding path.

The sun was still warm and the day crystal clear when they reached the top. The lighthouse was also a museum; but they did not go in. They stood under the sapphire sky and took in the magnificent, panoramic views of Africa's most southern tip. The continent starts many thousands of miles to the north and stretches down to cover great expanses of land, magnificent mountain ranges, raging rivers, and unforgiving deserts. Along its way and for millennia it has endowed some with fortune and punished others with famine, until it could wield its natural powers no further and kneeled down exhausted in the waters of the Indian and Atlantic oceans.

"The Rules of the Game," Sam said softly, under his breath, "is the palette with which Aaron showed me to paint my picture of choice. If I don't like what is on my canvas, I have the freedom to change it. I discover myself daily through conscious living and constant observation, living in the moment. The Rules of the Game are the keys to understanding ourselves first, then Life, and finally, God. In that order. Aaron showed me that."

She leaned with her back against him, his arms around her waist. They looked at the forlorn remains of a fishing vessel, just west of the lighthouse, capsized and dragged by treacherous currents into the shallow waters of the beach, creating the illusion of having given up on the sea and planning to make its escape over land.

"If we don't have clarity of who we are or where we are going, then the same fate awaits us as the Meisho Maru," Sam nodded his head in the direction of the Japanese wreck. "Like that ship, we'll be stuck, unable to move, and we'll have to watch with frustration as other ships that set their course effectively pass us by. But if we could learn from your magical birds," he turned her around so he could look at her, "to establish inner direction, we'd perhaps circle a few times in the sky, but inevitably, we'd head straight home."

Karla looked at him, this new man whom she was getting to know all over again. She thought of little Phoebe, of the mountain and the abyss that almost took Sam away, and then she thought of Aaron. She knew he was the key, but he was still a mystery to her. She saw the same peace in Sam's eyes as she felt in his presence and in his touch. She moved closer to him, and put her open palms on either side of his chest. Then she stood on her toes, reaching toward him.

Sam watched her with interest and amusement, realizing she was cleverly mimicking her childhood stance at the birdcage. He smiled knowingly. "What do you want to see, Karla?"

"What you see," she said simply. "Will you show me?"

Sam looked at her for a long moment; while his thoughts briefly drifted back to Aaron. "Of course," he said softly, gathering her in his arms.

"Sam, do you know who Aaron is?" she asked with her face against his chest.

Did he know who Aaron was? He remembered how annoyed he was when they first met. Then he became intrigued with his knowledge and insight, and started enjoying his company. That's when he began to learn from him. But did he know who he was?

"Sam?"

"Yes, I know." Then he laughed a wonderful, free laugh that resonated from his very soul. "Come Karla, let us go home. This beach has the same trait as the mountain; it dons a cloak of fog at night."

▲   ▲   ▲

In Closing

*T*hank you for coming along on the journey. I hope that you will continue to grow and that you will always remember that your life is your responsibility.

In the story you just completed, Aaron told Sam to write a book. The book you are holding in your hands is that book. It is important that you realize that this is not an autobiography. The story around *Stop Struggling and Start Living* is simply the medium I chose to share what I know with others.

To accompany this book is *Ten Truths From the Top of Table Mountain*, a step-by-step workbook of how to implement the Rules of the Game *into our daily lives*. It is available as an e-book that you can download from the publisher's website, www.dreamtimepublishing.com/books.php.

To reach a wider audience, I will also be hosting teleseminars. If you would like to participate, keep an eye on elfredapretorius.com. Dates and times of these events will be announced there.

▲ ▲ ▲

About the Author

Elfreda Pretorius has been actively involved in training, professional coaching, and public speaking for more than twenty years.

Stop Struggling and Start Living is the fruit of a lifetime of reading, studying, research, and personal experience, fueled by an insatiable quest for knowledge of the esoteric and spiritual world.

Her knowledge and experience now benefit those who seek her out for private counseling, or attend seminars she leads individually or in conjunction with other professionals.

Elfreda's love for writing began in her childhood. Her work has been published in several magazines including *Avatar* and *Personal Excellence* in the United states, and the Bay Street Bull in Toronto, Canada. Elfreda only recently decided to share her insights and perception with wider audiences by authoring *Stop Struggling and Start Living*.

She has in-depth knowledge of the information she shares with her audiences, underscored by a life-changing experience in coaching a critically injured child back from the brink of death by applying the principles of the *Stop Struggling and Start Living*. The story of his miraculous recovery is the subject of her next book.

A certified hypnotherapist and an expert in the functioning of the human psyche, she maintains that the average person can have far better control over the complexities of his or her personal and professional life. By understanding the Rules of the Game we can gain a measure of mastery previously thought impossible.

Elfreda was born in Cape Town, South Africa, but since 1994 has made her home in Ontario, Canada, where she lives with her husband and three sons. She continues to write and teach.

▲   ▲   ▲